THE BEST OF
Glasgow
CITY GUIDE & COOKBOOK

Merry Christmas '20
Kitty
May 2021 be filled with
fun discoveries
&
Adventure !
Lots of love,
Dad & Polly xxx

Glasgowist

The Best of Glasgow

©Glasgowist Ltd. All rights reserved.
First edition printed in 2020 in the UK.

ISBN 978-1-5272-7310-8

Published by Glasgowist in collaboration with
heraldscotland.com

The Herald

Supported by
The Glenlivet Single Malt Whisky

THE GLENLIVET.

By Paul Trainer

Art Director Ian Corcoran
Photographer Brian Sweeney
Additional photography Newsquest,
Glasgow Life, Sonya Walos, Paul Gallagher

Cover Design & Illustration Moona Paldanius

Contributors Paul English, David Kirkwood,
Madeleine Dunne, Rosalind Erskine,
Lynn Ferguson, Beverley Lyons, Kieran Adie,
Amy Lyall, Islay Raimund, Aline Browers

'My Glasgow' contributors Alex Kapranos,
Clare Grogan, Orde Meikle, Stuart McMillan,
PJ Moore, Pat Kane, Andy Cameron, Alan
McGee, Jean Johansson, Lynn Ferguson

Thanks to David Ward, Darren Blackburn,
Mike Phillips, David Ross, Nicola Moir,
Chad Davidson, Donald Martin, Callum Baird

Email hello@glasgowist.com

Printed in Great Britain
by Bell and Bain Glasgow Ltd

No part of this publication may be re-sold, reproduced or
transmitted in any form or by any means, electrical or mechanical,
including photocopying, scanning, recording or by any information
and storage retrieval system, without prior consent of the author
and publisher.

Although every precaution has been taken in the preparation of
this work, the publisher and author assume no responsibility for
errors or omissions. Neither is any liability assumed for damages
resulting from the use of the information contained within.

Old City, New Dreams

This book is an invitation to get to know Glasgow better. If you live here, you will find familiar landmarks to explore and new recommendations to discover. If you are far away, let our stories connect you to the life of the city. The Best of Glasgow is the culmination of five years of conversations and writing at Glasgowist.com. I started the website as a way to reconnect after spending a decade working for magazines in other cities. It's since grown into an active online community. One sunny day during lockdown, I started to bring together some of the people and places that deserve to be celebrated on these pages.

This year will be remembered for challenges and missed opportunities. It should also be remembered for a determined and resilient response, for the music and art that have been made, the food and drink places that are still at the heart of our communities, local businesses and new creatives looking to the future. Within this book you will find memories and nostalgia, but also take this as a declaration of intent for next year and beyond. There's a lot going on about the town. As long as there are people willing to work together and build their own dreams, then Glasgow will continue to flourish.

At the back of this book you will find recipes from some of our favourite restaurants and cafes. Try them at home to get a real taste of Glasgow.

Thank you to everyone who made this project possible, my friends, family, and anyone who makes the city a more interesting place to live. I'd like to dedicate this book to someone who continues to be part of my local story: my granda, Bill Hendry. See you at Coia's Cafe.

Paul Trainer
Glasgowist.com

Contents

GLASGOW'S TOP 20
ATTRACTIONS

1 Kelvingrove Art Gallery & Museum

Generations of Glasgow kids have slid across the marble floor of the Centre Hall on their knees, beneath the grand pipe organ that is still used for lunchtime recitals. Built in a Spanish Baroque style, there's a sense of magic to the place, beyond the collection of exhibits that includes outstanding artworks by Monet, Renoir and van Gogh. It opened in 1901, for the Glasgow International Exhibition held in Kelvingrove Park – taxi drivers will tell you the building is the wrong way round but that's an urban myth. Visit to see a Spitfire suspended from the ceiling above a stuffed elephant, furniture by Charles Rennie Mackintosh, collections of armour and the enigmatic presence of Salvador Dali's Christ of St John of the Cross. There's no doubt Glaswegians have a tangible sense of connection to the Kelvingrove. It belongs to them. Included in the latest Lonely Planet Ultimate Travel List.

📍 Argyle Street, G3 8AG 📞 0141 276 9599
📷 glasgowkelvingrove

2 Riverside Museum

Get a sense of where the city is coming from, and where it's going. The transport museum started when someone had the foresight to decide some of Glasgow's trams should be preserved after they stopped running. In an odd moment of synchronicity, the collection opening coincided with a wave of closures at shipyards on the Clyde with some 250 ship models soon finding a new home, then came hulking locomotives representing the city's railway heritage. You'll find the oldest surviving pedal cycle and a collection of Scottish-built cars and trucks. Look out for the Star Wars figures cabinet. A meticulously assembled street scene allows you to step into Glasgow of the past. The purpose-built museum, designed by Zaha Hadid, replaced the previous home for the collection at the Kelvin Hall.

📍 100 Pointhouse Road, G3 8RS 📞 0141 287 2720
📷 riversidemuseum

3 Glasgow Cathedral & Necropolis

The oldest building in the city marks the site where St Mungo is thought to have been buried in 612 AD. Its soaring Scottish Gothic architecture took shape between the 13th and 15th Centuries. Sir Walter Scott references the High Kirk in his novel, Rob

Roy. More recently the cathedral has found new fame as a backdrop in the television show Outlander. It will also feature in the forthcoming Batman movie starring Robert Pattinson, alongside the nearby Necropolis, that can be reached by crossing the Bridge of Sighs, part of the funeral procession route. Glasgow's city of the dead, the Necropolis cemetery is a remarkable Victorian display "dedicated to the genius of memory".

📍 Castle St, G4 0QZ

4 The Mitchell Library

The foundation stone was laid by Andrew Carnegie in 1907. A collection of over a million books and photographs is housed across a majestic building with a distinctive copper dome and a 1970s extension with wonderfully kitsch carpets. There's a comfy cafe on the ground floor. The Mitchell holds the Glasgow City Archives and Special Collections including Robert Burns hand-written manuscripts. The theatre here hosts events during the Aye Write! literary festival.

📍 North Street, G3 7DN 📞 0141 287 2999
🌐 mitchelllibrary.org

5 City Chambers

The headquarters of successive councils since 1889, City Chambers looms large over the eastern side of George Square. Public tours are conducted twice a day. Its marble staircase is reputed to be the biggest in Western Europe and has featured in films as a stand in for the Kremlin and the Vatican. The Banqueting Hall is where figures including President Ulysses S Grant, Marie Curie, Nelson Mandela and Sir Alex Ferguson were given the Freedom of the City. The walls are decorated with murals showing some of the history of the city. The artists were from the Glasgow School including Sir John Lavery, Alexander Roche and George Henry.

📍 George Square, G2 1DU
🌐 glasgow.gov.uk

6 The People's Palace and Glasgow Green

A cultural centre for the East End and a repository of folk memory. At the opening ceremony, Lord Rosebery introduced: "A palace of pleasure and

City Chambers

imagination around which the people may place their affections and which may give them a home on which their memory may rest" which is pretty much how things have worked out. The Winter Gardens are currently closed which is a matter of much consternation. The collection includes pictures and depictions of working class Glasgow life through the ages, particularly in the 20th Century, with a one-room tenement home and memorabilia from the Barrowland Ballroom. Billy Connolly's banana boots are one of the most popular exhibits. The Doulton Fountain outside is the biggest terracotta fountain in the world. It sits on the border of Glasgow Green, the oldest park in the city.

📍 Templeton Street, G40 1AT 📞 0141 276 0788

7 Theatre Royal

The oldest theatre in Glasgow – it opened in 1867 – and the longest running in Scotland. In 1957 it became the Scottish Television Theatre and served as TV studios for the newly formed STV. It is now

the home of Scottish Opera and Scottish Ballet. A modern refurbishment created a new stylish foyer and curved extension, but the venue retains its Victorian auditorium and sense of history.

📍 282 Hope Street, G2 3QA

8 Glasgow Science Centre

Part of the redeveloped Glasgow Garden Festival site on the south bank of the Clyde. The Glasgow Tower at the complex is the tallest tower in Scotland. Its observation deck operates between April and October. The Science Centre regularly features in broadcasts by near neighbours at Pacific Quay BBC Scotland and STV. There are interactive exhibits to discover including a planetarium and a workshop space.

📍 50 Pacific Quay, G51 1EA 📞 0141 420 5000
🌐 glasgowsciencecentre.org

9 Scotland Street Museum

Designed by Charles Rennie Mackintosh between 1903-1906 for the School Board of Glasgow, it arrived over budget and was considered an extravagance with a pair of windowed Scottish baronial style tours and design cues from Rowallan Castle and Falkland Palace. Now, it is considered one of the city's greatest architectural attractions, particularly after the fire at the Art School. As a museum of education, visitors can interact with actors telling stories from the Victorian era through to the late 20th Century.

📍 225 Scotland Street, G5 8QB 📞 0141 287 0500

Pollok House

COLIN MEARNS

10 Pollok House

The ancestral home of the Maxwell family, the present house dates from 1752 and contains one of the finest collections of Spanish art in the country alongside Edwardian furnishings. The discussions for the founding of the National Trust for Scotland took place inside Pollok House's cedar-panelled smoking room. Its elegant gardens add to the country park setting.

📍 Pollok Country Park, G43 1AT
🌐 nts.org.uk/pollok-house

11 Scottish Football Museum

Discover the Hampden Roar and get to the heart of Glasgow's football soul. The stadium tour let's you experience the stadium the way players do on match day. The museum has one of the old turnstiles and the original dressing room from Hampden. There's the original Scottish Cup. The Scottish Football Hall of Fame features memorabilia relating to players like Denis Law, Jim Baxter and Kenny Dalglish.

📍 Hampden Park, G42 9BA 📞 0141 616 6139
🌐 scottishfootballmuseum.org.uk

12 The Govan Stones

A fascinating collection of early medieval stones carved in the 9th-11th Centuries is housed in the

atmospheric surroundings of Govan Old Parish Church. The Govan Sarcophagus is the only one of its kind carved from solid stone from pre-Norman northern Britain. The churchyard is not done giving up its secrets. Last year, a community archaeology dig uncovered long-lost gravestones from the Middle Ages featuring Celtic interlace designs to commemorate the Kings of Strathclyde.

📍 866 Govan Road, G51 3DL
🌐 thegovanstones.org.uk

13 The Lighthouse

The Lighthouse is Scotland's Centre for Design and Architecture, placed in the former offices of the

Glasgow Herald newspaper, designed by Charles Rennie Mackintosh. The imposing, vast edifice is hidden in plain sight on Mitchell Lane. Today, it is home to permanent and temporary exhibitions. One of its best features are the uninterrupted views over Glasgow's cityscape from the Mackintosh Tower at the north of the building and its helical staircase.

📍 11 Mitchell Lane, G1 3NU
🌐 thelighthouse.co.uk

14 Drygate and Tennent's Brewery

A microbrewery, bar and kitchen sitting alongside a brewery, bar and visitor centre. Drygate and Tennent's Brewery stand together as two very different experiences that together tell the story of local beer. The Heritage Centre at Tennent's Brewery introduces the history of Scotland's most popular lager through the ages, bringing in elements of Glasgow folk history and the story of the city's pubs. It all ends up with a pint of Big Juicy at the end. Follow the mural wall round the corner and meet Drygate with their brewhouse in a stripped-back industrial setting. Ask for a beer flight selection to get to know the place, order a pie and make yourself comfortable. Cheers to a great day out.

📍 85 Drygate, G4 0UT 📞 0141 212 8815
🌐 drygate.com

15 Crookston Castle

Glasgow's only surviving medieval castle which retains some distinctive features including its north east tower. Its origins date back to a fortification built by Sir Robert de Croc in the late 1100s. The property passed to the Stewart family and was besieged during the struggle to establish control over the future of the infant Mary, Queen of Scots. Two decades later it is thought that Mary agreed to marry Lord Darnley here. The castle featured in Frankie Boyle's Tour of Scotland.

📍 170 Brockburn Road, G53 5RY

16 The Tenement House

A snapshot of early 20th Century life, captured in a four-room flat. The Tenement House was the home of Miss Agnes Toward, a shorthand typist, and her mother from 1911 until 1965. The fixtures and fittings remained unchanged in over half a century and the tenement now lives on as a time capsule exhibition.

📍 145 Buccleuch Street, G3 6QN 📞 0141 333 0183

17 Central Station

Glasgow Central Station was opened by the Caledonian Railway in 1879 on the north bank of the Clyde. As well as being the busiest train station in the city it is a landmark in its own right, including the Heilanman's Umbrella canopy over Argyle Street, so named because displaced highlanders would arrange to meet up there at weekends.

The first long distance television pictures transmitted in the UK were sent to Central Station in 1927. The station tour takes you through subterranean passageways beneath the streets to visit railway vaults connected to Glasgow's industrial expansion.

📍 Gordon Street, G1 3SL
🌐 glasgowcentraltours.co.uk

18 Britannia Panopticon

The world's oldest surviving music hall. At one time a boisterous crowd of up to 1500 would gather to watch the singers, dancers and comedians. Eccentric showman A.E. Pickard installed a carnival in the attic and a zoo in the basement.

Now, a charitable group promotes the legacy of building and continues to organise events, including silent movie screenings. Stan Laurel made his debut on this stage in 1906.

📍 113-117 Trongate, G1 5HD 📞 0141 553 0840
🌐 britanniapanopticon.org

19 GoMA

One of the most photographed buildings in the city, mostly because of the statue of the Duke of Wellington in front of it that acquired a traffic cone in the early 80s. Offer your own interpretation of this community art installation to passing tourists. Exhibits in GoMA include works by David Hockney and Andy Warhol. Glasgow has produced five Turner Prize artists since the gallery opened in 1996.

📍 Royal Exchange Square, G1 3AF

20 Botanic Gardens

Sitting at the junction of Great Western Road and Byres Road, overlooked by Oran Mor, the Botanics is a much-loved bit of West End greenery. It features several glasshouses, the biggest of which is the Kibble Palace – a wrought-iron framed glasshouse designed for John Kibble and moved here in 1873 – which houses the UK's national collection of tree ferns. In recent years the gardens have hosted itison's GlasGLOW Halloween festival and a regular book market. There's an old Tardis-style police box outside the gates that's home to a tiny coffee takeaway.

📍 730 Great Western Road, G12 0UE
🌐 glasgowbotanicgardens.com

Botanic Gardens

JAMIE SIMPSON

GLASGOW'S TOP 20
RESTAURANTS

The Gannet

1 The Gannet

The menu remains dominated by exceptional Scottish produce, served with precision. If anything, the kitchen seems to have stepped things up a notch this year despite the challenges that has faced the industry as a whole. What a performance you get across lunch at The Gannet. That's what we are here for: A restaurant with a sense of occasion balanced with good humour and enthusiasm.

We start off with west coast crab punctuated by slivers of parsnip and apple. Aged Taylor's of Heatheryhall shorthorn beef carpaccio served with kohlrabi, smoked eel, potato is an eye-catching signature dish. Then comes the double-hit of North Sea monkfish and celeriac in a seaweed butter sauce followed by saddle of Cairngorm red deer accompanied by beetroot, wild Argyll mushrooms and elderberry. As close to an ideal selection of Scottish produce as you will find. A real triumph.

Special mention for the optional cheese course, a frothy, light textured serving of Winslade with buckwheat and plums – which we later find out were grown by kids from nearby Woodside primary. Dessert brings things to a crescendo with smoked chocolate, blackberry and sea buckthorn.

The Gannet has consistently led from the front during the five years Glasgowist has charted local food and drink.

Best Dish: Saddle of red deer as part of the seasonal set menu (£50).

📍 1155 Argyle Street, G3 8TB 📞 0141 204 2081
🌐 thegannetgla.com

2 Gamba

As soon as Derek Marshall found himself working in a kitchen, he knew that's where he wanted to be. A commitment to preparing the best seafood available has seen Gamba through two

decades of two AA Rosette ratings, establishing a modern Glasgow classic. "I just love seeing clean plates coming back to the kitchen when you know someone has enjoyed their meal. Our portions are quite substantial, you'll get a real feed here" he says. Derek had previously been head chef at Rogano and then Papingo, with culinary journeys to France and Spain before opening Gamba in 1998. His favourite cuisine is Japanese food, so you see ingredients like soy, ginger and lemongrass enliven a menu that has an adventurous, independent spirit. An utterly consistent gem, they do amazing things with king scallops and mussels.

Best Dish: Isle of Gigha halibut, sweetcorn, peat smoked haddock, torched tomatoes, garden peas (£25)

📍 225A W George Street, G2 2ND 📞 0141 572 0899
🌐 gamba.co.uk

3 Ka Pao

Housed in the basement of the Botanic Gardens Garage, Ka Pao is a modern, bright, stylish space for 120 covers across an open dining room, with a custom-designed kitchen and a bar area featuring comfortable booths and high tables. A spin-off from Ox and Finch, it's been a smash hit since opening at the start of the year. Owner and chef Jonathan MacDonald was inspired to do something different by food he experienced when he was a young chef: "I spent quite a lot of time travelling in my 20s in Southeast Asia, it blew my socks off. Eating chilli crab cakes in car parks. Real street food. I was mesmerised by it all, especially when I lived and worked in Melbourne." Always order the spicy caramel fried chicken.

Best Dish: Corn ribs, salted coconut, shrimp and lime (£4.50)

📍 26 Vinicombe Street, G12 8BE 📞 0141 483 6990
🌐 kapaogla.com

4 Glaschu

An exciting new addition to the local food scene – modern Scottish fine dining within The Western Club building on Royal Exchange Square. Head chef Dion Scott honed his skills in Heston Blumenthal's kitchens. Despite the stop-start nature of local hospitality this year, they've established signature dishes like beef Wellington or lobster and langoustine cannelloni while attracting a stylish crowd. The restaurant draws its identity from its position in a landmark location, with nods to local history and culture throughout the menu. The added element is an international approach to food that elevates the overall experience. Set to be a new brunch destination on weekends.

Best Dish: Fillet of hake, confit potatoes, buttered kale, Bourguignon garnish from the market menu (£25 for three courses)

📍 32 Royal Exchange Sq, G1 3AB 📞 0141 248 2214
🌐 glaschurestaurant.co.uk

5 Ox and Finch

What makes Ox and Finch great is the way the chefs operate as a collective. The menu is always brimming with new ideas that have been fine tuned to be part of the small plate offering. The team takes pride in their work and a collegial sense of competitiveness keeps things moving in the right direction. The fact that the kitchen can maintain impeccably high standards across a menu that covers a vast swathe of culinary ground is testament to the talent here. Expect a lively neighbourhood restaurant atmosphere. Assemble a colourful collection of dishes: Divide and conquer.

Best Dish: Cod cheeks, chorizo, tomato and morcilla on toasted sourdough (£7.50)

📍 920 Sauchiehall Street, G3 7TF 📞 0141 339 8627
🌐 oxandfinch.com

Ka Pao

6 Lychee Oriental

In chef and owner Jimmy Lee's kitchen, Scottish ingredients are transformed by Cantonese spices and cooking techniques. He has a strong sense of connection with his restaurant regulars, who treat this place like it's their home: "I'm basically here all the time, I want to make sure everything is right. Through the business, I've made so many friends, just getting to know people from them visiting and enjoying the food. It's a very Glasgow thing, I think." The menu is compact, focusing on key dishes and retaining a depth of flavour.
Best Dish: Twice cooked pork belly with spicy black bean sauce (£14.90)
📍 59 Mitchell Street, G1 3LN ☎ 0141 248 2240
🌐 lycheeoriental.co.uk

7 Cail Bruich

It was the signing of the season: chef Lorna McNee *(below)*, protégé of the late two Michelin starred chef, Andrew Fairlie and last year's Great British Menu Champion of Champions took up her

first head chef role at Cail Bruich in August, joining from Restaurant Andrew Fairlie. This meant co-owner Chris Charalambous stepped away from the kitchen for the first time since the restaurant opened in 2008. Dishes on her inaugural menus included: West coast crab, raw Orkney scallop and citrus alongside hand rolled pasta, broad beans, girolles and truffle.
Best Dish: Scrabster halibut, grape, verjus sauce as part of the four-course tasting menu (£65)
📍 725 Great Western Rd, G12 8QX ☎ 0141 334 6265
🌐 cailbruich.co.uk

8 Six by Nico

Chef Nico Simeone has taken his dining concept across the country, opening in Edinburgh, Belfast, Manchester, Liverpool and, most recently, in London.

There's also the Southside outpost on Nithsdale Road, but it all started here on Argyle Street. They tell a different story through food every six weeks. A new six course menu is announced, inspired by a place or a memory. Experimental preparations cue nostalgic emotions, deconstruct a particular cuisine or pepper a series of small plates with pop culture references. The whole experience is fun, playful and challenges expectations. After time runs out on one theme, the culinary team simply moves on to the next set of flavours. Home dining is set to be a future focus for the business with a new distribution base in Anniesland. Paolo Nutini is a fan.
Best Dish: Six course tasting menu (£29)
📍 1132 Argyle Street, G3 8TD ☎ 0141 334 5661
🌐 sixbynico.co.uk

9 Brian Maule at Chardon d'Or

After Brian Maule left school, he decided he wanted to learn to be a chef so set off with a couple of pals to find work in Lyon. "France was a massive influence on me in terms of understanding produce. There's work that's gone into these individual ingredients, and there's somebody making that effort. You show respect to ingredients. There was also an understanding of discipline. Learning not just how to cook but finding who you are and how strong you are as a person." The rising star was then appointed head chef at the world-famous Michelin star Le Gavroche in London. He returned home to open his own restaurant in 2001, the fulfilment of a lifelong dream. His restaurant is an important culinary marker for Glasgow, somewhere you can expect the highest standard of fine dining and service.
Best Dish: Fillet of Scotch lamb, crushed peas, rosemary jus (£34.50)
📍 176 West Regent Street, G2 4RL ☎ 0141 248 3801
🌐 brianmaule.com

10 One Devonshire Gardens

One Devonshire Gardens is the restaurant within the boutique Hotel du Vin that occupies a handsome row of townhouses just off Great Western Road. It has a rich tradition of fine dining and discreet hospitality, retaining its own identity. Since the arrival of head chef Gary Townsend, with over 17 years of experience in some of the country's top kitchens, including Restaurant Martin Wishart and Cameron House, an evening here is an impressive experience. Gary says: "We have a fantastic larder here in Scotland and you'll find this in each of my menus. We are extremely fortunate to have, in my opinion, the best seafood on the planet and this is showcased through dishes

Brian Maule at Chardon d'Or

including salmon, scallops and lemon sole." The three course Sunday lunch is a local tradition.

Best Dish: Wood pigeon, celeriac, chicory, nuts and seeds as part of the tasting menu (£69 per person)

📍 1 Devonshire Gardens, G12 0UX 📞 0141 378 0385

📷 hotelduvinglasgow

11 Bilson Eleven

Nick Rietz and his wife Liz set out to open a small but ambitious restaurant in a townhouse on Annfield Place. Three years later, they have firmly established fine dining in Dennistoun. Nick likes to create his own interpretation of Scottish dishes and has a kitchen garden for ingredient inspiration. He says: "Bilson Eleven is intimate, informal dining, where our focus is always on quality rather than quantity. Our aim is to give exceptional food and service to a smaller-scale customer base – we want to make sure that every person who dines here is given a totally unique experience."

Presentation and the story behind the food is important here. They are currently offering a nine-course seasonal tasting menu, adding layers to the meal, dish by dish, served in comfortable, homely surroundings. This year Bilson Eleven has rolled with the times, creating home dining set menus with options like shellfish bisque or truffle mac 'n' cheese.

Best Dish: Cured Loch Etive trout as part of the tasting menu (£79 per person)

📍 10 Annfield Place, G31 2XQ 📞 0141 554 6259

🌐 bilsoneleven.co.uk

12 Julie's Kopitiam

A Shawlands favourite, Julie Lin MacLeod's Kopitiam is one of the busiest food places in a particularly competitive part of Glasgow's culinary map. Much of the appeal comes from colourful, simple dishes that are packed with flavour. This year has seen the team return to their street food roots with spin-off brand Ga-Ga Chicken becoming part of the offering at SWG3's outdoor food yard. They are currently offering a dining at home menu.

Best Dish: Nasi Goreng (£9)

📍 1109 Pollokshaws Road, G41 3YG 📞 0141 237 9560

🌐 julieskopitiam.com

13 The Dhabba

Chef JD Tewari has cooked for ministerial and presidential banquets as well as being a personal chef to the Prime Minister of India. You'll now find him in charge of the kitchen at The Dhabba, where they create North Indian cuisine

inspired by traditional roadside diners for this entertaining restaurant on Candleriggs. Owner Navdeep Basi says: "We have found over the years that people in Glasgow are interested in trying out new tastes. There are dishes on our menu that people really respond to like our lamb bhoona gosht. People are well travelled and interested in authentic flavours." The Dhabba caters for vegans and all their recipes are nut free. Sister restaurant Dakhin serves gluten free south Indian cuisine.

Best Dish: Achari Tikka (£13.95)

📍 44 Candleriggs, G1 1LD 📞 0141 553 1249

🌐 thedhabba.com

14 Ubiquitous Chip

This Ashton Lane landmark's enduring appeal is a combination of outstanding local ingredients, prepared with flair, and the atmosphere generated by an enthusiastic bunch of bohemian customers. Owner and chef Colin Clydesdale was raised in restaurants – his father Ronnie opened The Chip in 1971, while Colin went on to start another West End favourite at Stravaigin and he also has

Hanoi Bike Shop on Ruthven Lane. Expect Hebridean crab, Shetland mussels and Loch Etive sea trout, alongside game from Scottish estates. They also have a vegetarian tasting menu.

Best Dish: The Chip's own venison haggis, potato purée, whisky glazed neep (£9)

📍 12 Ashton Lane, G12 8SJ 📞 0141 334 5007

🌐 ubiquitouschip.co.uk

15 Mother India

Mother India has been on the frontline of representing Glasgow food since they opened in 1990 aiming to serve Indian home cooking in a restaurant setting at affordable prices. Mother India's Cafe opened next door in 2004 where you can enjoy small plates and vegetable dishes with samosas, pakoras and

paneer. A West End favourite and standard bearer for local curries. Start with a ginger crab and prawn dosa.

Best Dish: Smoked lamb with broccoli and green chilli (£13.50)

📍 28 Westminster Terrace, G3 7RU 📞 0141 221 1663

🌐 motherindia.co.uk

16 Little Hoi An

Creating a stir in Strathbungo, this tiny Vietnamese street food place has been a sensation since opening on Allison Street. Big flavours and a lot of fun in a cosy setting. They are having great success as a takeaway at the moment. Load up on crispy minced pork pancake rolls, homemade dumplings and wok fried flat rice noodles.

Best Dish: Salt n chilli pork with sticky sauce (£9.80)

📍 26 Allison Street, G42 8NN 📞 0141 424 1114
📷 littlehoian_glasgow

17 Cafe Gandolfi

PJ Moore tells us that when he was touring with The Blue Nile, part of his ritual for returning to Glasgow was to get a taxi straight to Cafe Gandolfi. It's an important place in the local food story – mentioned more than any other when we speak to folk about their restaurant memories. The dining room is a work of art. The food continues to represent the best of modern Scottish cooking. Fun fact: Those distinctive revolving doors at the entrance are over 100 years old and were once part of the Grand Hotel at Charing Cross until it was demolished. They were installed here in 1969. Recently, the bar upstairs has been used for pop-up events and innovative seafood and cocktail pairing menus. A city centre food place to be cherished. You won't find it anywhere else.

Best Dish: Peat smoked haddock, crushed potatoes, mustard cream, poached egg (£16.50)

📍 84-86 Albion Street, G1 1NY 📞 0141 552 9475
🌐 cafegandolfi.com

18 La Lanterna

Charismatic chef Luca Conreno brings big flavours straight from Italy to his Hope Street and Great Western Road restaurants. Think risotto, rigatoni and lobster ravioli. Luca is a familiar sight in his own dining room, taking time out of the kitchen to chat: "I like the communication with customers. A restaurant is a social place." They make the best carbonara in Glasgow and have a passion for what they do. Kevin Bridges and Peter Mullan are fans. Celebrating 50 years in business this year.

Best Dish: Spaghetti Arragosta (£15.95)

📍 447 Great Western Rd, G12 8HH 📞 0141 334 0686
🌐 lalanternawestend.co.uk

19 The Butchershop Bar and Grill

Popular for date night, The Butchershop is a neighbourhood grill with a devoted following. Go for prime cuts of grass-fed Scotch beef, hung on the bone and dry-aged for up to 45 days.

Enjoy with hand-cut chips and macaroni cheese on the side. Outstanding local produce, prepared with skill and precision. Grab a booth with a view of the Kelvingrove. A sister restaurant of The Spanish Butcher in town.

Best Dish: Tomahawk steak (£8 per 100 grams)

📍 1055 Sauchiehall Street, G3 7UD 📞 0141 339 2999
🌐 butchershopglasgow.com

20 Crabshakk

Crabshakk kickstarted the Finnieston food and drink boom when they opened in 2009. Oysters, a cracking fish supper and their Fruits de Mer platter have been on the menu since day one. Study the specials board which changes twice a day. We usually look for grilled langoustines. Glasgow has access to a dazzling supply of fresh seafood and here the flavours are showcased in a compact, cool restaurant with a laid-back vibe and cheerful service.

Best Dish: Seared scallops with anchovies (£9.95)

📍 1114 Argyle Street, G3 8TD 📞 0141 334 6127
🌐 crabshakk.com

Crabshakk

City Chambers

Public tours are conducted twice a day. Its marble staircase is reputed to be the biggest in Western Europe and has featured in films as a stand in for the Kremlin and the Vatican.

GLASGOW'S TOP 20

BARS

The Gate

1 The Gate

Andy Gemmell created The Gate within an unassuming building across from the Barrowland Ballroom. You enter through the original close before the room is revealed, an impressive, comfortable mix of the old and the new.

Andy says "I wanted to create somewhere that everyone's going to understand and feel welcome when they come in." The idea was to fuse his enthusiasm for traditional Scottish pubs with influences from the worlds' best cocktail venues, some of which he visited while working as a whisky ambassador.

Wherever you sit, your eye is drawn to the bar itself where the team are meticulously making their drinks. A new cocktail list is introduced every six weeks. It's a sociable space where market traders have a pint sitting alongside established whisky aficionados and a fashionable new generation. Framed pictures of local characters by

Glasgow photographer Mark Leslie on the wall give the bar a sense of place.
📍 251 Gallowgate, G4 0TP 📞 07852 636 764
🌐 thegateglasgow.com

2 Tabac

A world of influences coalesce in this classy drinking den on Mitchell Lane. Take a table by the window for a spot of people-watching. To your right, as you arrive in the door, they have added a neat

bar with organic wine available by the glass. Their Black Rose cocktail is Cocchi Torino vermouth, Chambord and homemade rosemary syrup, shaken up and served straight. Much of the distinctive interior remains from when this was Bar Ten, "Scotland's first style bar", that opened in 1991, designed by Ben Kelly who was also responsible for designing Manchester's Haçienda nightclub. Popular for Tinder dates during the week. Progressive music policy, good chat and strong drinks at the weekend.
📍 10 Mitchell Lane, G1 3NU 📞 0141 572 1448
🌐 tabacbar.com

3 Kelvingrove Cafe

Kelvingrove Café claimed this corner of Argyle Street in 2013 just as an overlooked stretch of the West End found a new lease of life. Owner Barry Oattes believes they assumed their role in the area quickly: "It always felt like a great neighbourhood. There were interesting people around, folk who were proud of the area. It just needed a gang hut. A clubhouse for everyone. That's what we wanted to be and that's how it has worked out." The bar and brasserie has become a fixed point amidst a local scene that revels in change and new arrivals.

Closure this year allowed them to complete their plans to transform the familiar venue, extending the ground floor with the

addition of a new 240 sq ft dining room. The new space features Versailles panel tables, pine green Spanish plaster walls and imported Italian terracotta floor tiles – as well as a huge Crittall steel-framed window,

an addition that allows light to flood into the dining room. The bar and brasserie returns with a renewed focus on cocktails, brunch, sharing plates and good times.

Kelvingrove Café was an ice cream parlour when it opened in 1896, then lay abandoned before being reimaged as a stylish place for drinks. In homage to the history of the building, their new menu features desserts devised by Minted ice cream on Byres Road including a traditional knickerbocker glory, peach Melba and banana split. We love the painting of the Rolling Stones by the door.
📍 1161 Argyle Street, G3 8TB 📞 0141 221 8988
🌐 kelvingrovecafe.com

4 The Locale

The creation of second-generation publican Josh Barr. They've got one of the biggest and most in-demand beer garden in the city where you'll find weekend barbecues and people wearing Wayfarer sunglasses drinking Aperol spritz. The bar itself draws from international influences. They make their own Limoncello and there's a New York style dive bar in the basement. Popular for brunch at the weekend.
📍 241 North St, G3 7DL 📞 0141 221 9036
🌐 thelocaleglasgow.com

5 Óran Mòr

Óran Mòr, within the stately surroundings of what was Kelvinside Parish Church, with its tall Gothic spire, was

---

Nightlife Voices Josh Barr, The Locale

Colin Barr is the man who launched Bennetts in the 80s, then The Tunnel and members-only club The Apartment in the 90s. He went on to open the Bier Halle in 1999, then his son Josh joined the business before opening his own fashionable venture The Locale.

"I started working weekends in the Bier Halle washing pots, then running my own kitchen at 17. As soon as I turned 18 I started pulling pints. I took time to study at Art School in Dundee but throughout that time I was promoting club nights so I can say I've been involved in the trade since I was 15.

"After returning from Art School I managed the Bier Halle, developed my ideas and concepts and kept learning as much as I could. That place was the best education I ever had. I started looking for premises and funding and with hard work and a little bit of good fortune, The Locale was born.

"I have always had a passion for graffiti and typography and still practice that to this day. My favourite piece of art in the bar is by my best mates from Art School, The Brownlee Brothers, and we have signage by The Unlikely Painter and Ciarán Glöbel. The yard has

a couple of decent walls that I like to ply my trade on and also I acquired a piece I painted over lockdown with my friend Scott Lister on ORO Italian in Shawlands, 'Stay Safe'.

"Becoming a publican was something I dreamed of, although I didn't always expect this is where my life would take me, I'm so glad to be where I'm at. My dad is my main inspiration, he leads a pretty good life and the apple doesn't fall far from the tree. The success of independent operators in Glasgow is inspiring. Glasgow people recognise the real ones. Be original and be bold."

saved from being turned into flats by Colin Beattie. He has not only created one of the great bars in the West End – a meeting place for pints and pals – but an important venue for art, culture and food.

📍 top of Byres Road, G12 8QX 📞 0141 357 6200
🌐 oran-mor.co.uk

6 The Pot Still

A fixture on Hope Street since 1867, The Pot Still since 1981 and run by the Murphy family since 2011. This pub is

the place for malt whisky in the city centre, with over 700 bottles loaded onto their bulging gantry. You'll also find cracking cask ales and proper pies. They host whisky tastings throughout the year or offer guidance whenever you feel like starting to explore some drams.

📍 154 Hope Street, G2 2TH 📞 0141 333 0980
🌐 thepotstill.co.uk

7 The Citizen

This imposing red brick building was once where copies of the Evening Citizen newspaper were prepared and printed. An impressive open space with high ceilings – spot pictures on the walls by Charles Hamilton, a street photographer who specialises in portraits. A feature of the main bar is the Tennent's Tank Lager system, the first time this way of delivering a pint has been used in Scotland since the 1980s. Sit at a booth at the front for the best view of the bar. A grand place to linger over drinks at the weekend.

📍 24 St Vincent Place, G1 2EU 📞 0141 222 2909
🌐 thecitizenglasgow.co.uk

8 The Laurieston

A time capsule of local hospitality. Embraced by music fans and hipster blow-ins who have joined lifelong residents. At its heart The Laurieston is a family-run

The Spiritualist

neighbourhood spot, with interiors that haven't changed since the 1960s.

The Laurieston's enduring charm comes from its distinctive look, a warm welcome and a strong sense of identity. Saoirse Ronan popped in for a pint with Jack Lowden, and Kieran Culkin filmed a scene here for an episode of Succession.

📍 58 Bridge Street, G5 9HU 📞 0141 429 4528
📷 laurestonbar

9 The Spiritualist

They like to put on a show with customised glassware, dry ice, surprising colour combinations and theatrical presentation at your table. You've probably seen them on Instagram. It's "cocktails to make you smile".

Order the Madame Marmalade: Bombay Sapphire gin, Solerno blood orange sugar syrup, orange marmalade, tonic and bitters.

Nightlife Voices Charles Fulton Asson, Barman at The Old Toll Bar

"If I have friends visiting, I always take them to the People's Palace, nothing represents Glasgow culture like it. Then we'd go to the Riverside Museum – it isn't just cars you know! My favourite part is taking a static ride on the old Clockwork Orange underground train carriage and meandering down the old cobble street of yesteryear.

Then I introduce them to the Old Toll Bar. What better place to end your day of sightseeing than enjoying a half and half under the candlelight of this listed beauty. The gantry is one of the youngest parts of the interior and even that is 130 years old.

In terms of food, having a Brummie father, South Asian cuisine was a staple in our house, and some-

thing I always crave. Kebabish Grill in Glasgow's Southside does it for me. If you want a dish to remember, go for the garlic chilli lamb, it's dynamite. I always find myself popping into Variety bar for a catch-up and decent tunes. When I was younger, I was a bit of a skater boy so I would go to the skate park at Kelvingrove. It can be tranquil and eventful in equal measure.

At the bar, we have worked with the ethos of the city, that 'can-do' attitude. Our concept for the bar was grassroots led. The bar was built around what the area was looking for. We spoke to hundreds of locals and asked what they wanted.

This is as much their place as it is ours.

Or how about a Rhubarbra Streisand: Absolut Vanilla vodka, Edinburgh Gin rhubarb and ginger liqueur, lemon juice, sugar syrup, topped with Irn Bru.

📍 62 Miller Street, G1 1DT 📞 0141 248 4165

🌐 thespiritualistglasgow.com

10 The Rum Shack

A place that has that little bit of random magic. A local bar for Southsiders with Caribbean sensibilities, created in a palette of red, green and yellow with more than a hundred rums available from all over the world.

The evening crowd is sprinkled with boho creatives, people in bands and people who look like they are in bands. You can also order dishes that pack a vibrant punch. They set a trend by creating a distinctive hangout in Govanhill.

📍 657 Pollokshaws Road, G41 2AB 📞 0141 237 4432

🌐 rumshackglasgow.com

11 Chinaskis

Named after the literary alter ego of writer Charles Bukowski but the theme is more defined by the cadre of regulars that have made this place their own. The bar boasts an impressive split-level terrace at the back.

Long established and quietly confident in its hip credentials. They stock a fine selection of rum. Bare stone walls, resident DJs, feature art, small plates and a laidback metropolitan style.

📍 239 North Street, G3 7DL 📞 0141 221 0061

🌐 chinaskis.com

12 The Amsterdam

Music is important at this dog-friendly, stylish city centre bar, with DJs at the weekends and an upbeat soundtrack most nights. Tom Walker hosted his aftershow party here and Lewis Capaldi is a fan. They have a freewheeling approach to a rotating cocktail selection.

An outside area for pints when it's sunny. Shakshuka baked eggs and a Bloody Mary for brunch. Elsewhere on the menu – burgers, loaded fries and sourdough pizza.

Soon to open a high-concept basement speakeasy bar that will be an exciting new addition to the city centre scene.

📍 106-108 Brunswick Street, G1 1TF 📞 0141 552 5108

🌐 thedamglasgow.com

13 The Sparkle Horse

A firm favourite with the community and headquarters for local musicians since opening in December 2012. They have another place, The Bell Jar in Govanhill. Both are very comfortable places to while away a couple of hours. The interior of The Sparkle Horse has been updated, but there are enough familiar throwbacks to make you think of the old bars in Peter McDougall dramas. West Brewery's St Mungo is on tap and there are 14 different wines available. Great fish and chips. They've been known to play albums in their entirety.

📍 16 Dowanhill Street, G11 5QS 📞 0141 562 3175

🌐 thesparklehorse.com

14 Nice N Sleazy

A real music landmark with a carefully crafted dive bar interior – they work hard at appearing louche but this is actually one of the best run places on Sauchiehall Street. Have a good time, but they'll stand for no nonsense. Expect a potent cocktail menu – a Buckaroo is Buckfast, creme de peche and lemonade – the muffled sound of a gig in the basement mixing with whatever album is on heavy rotation on the bar's playlist. Food is by Koko's Japanese Kitchen in the evening. Sleazy's have a great track record of street food and restaurant collaborations – students can't survive on guitar riffs and tequila shots alone. Usually rocking until 3am at weekends.

📍 421 Sauchiehall Street, G2 3LG 📞 0141 333 0900

🌐 nicensleazy.com

15 The Doublet

A Glasgow pub that found a moment in time and just decided to stay there. It wears it well. A reassuring fixed point in the West End,

always ready to offer a friendly welcome. It can look a bit frayed around the edges in places, but don't we all at this stage. Regulars wouldn't have it any other way. Go for cask ales and conversation. We like the timeless, homely appeal of the upstairs lounge.

📍 74 Park Road, G4 9JF 📞 0141 334 1982

⚬ thedoubletbar

16 Redmond's

The bar recently acquired a Dennistoun mural on its wall to match its emblematic status as a local hangout and community hub. A sister bar to Phillies of Shawlands, founded by brothers Conor and Luke Miskimmin. An independent spirit, great record collection and lots of local craft beers. We like their bao bun and gyoza bar snacks with our bourbon.

📍 304 Duke Street, G31 1RZ 📞 0141 572 5664

⚬ redmondsofdennistoun

Nice N Sleazy

Nightlife Voices Michael Grieve, Managing Director, Sub Club

Was becoming a club owner something you dreamed about at high school?
It was never a plan but I was always drawn towards the music industry and partying.

My cousin was married to the general manager of The Apollo in its heyday during the 70s when I was growing up and I was able to get into loads of gigs there and had a sneaky peek behind the scenes at times. That undoubtedly influenced my eventual career choice.

What's been the most significant influence on the Sub Club?
Harri has influenced the sound of the Subbie more than any other individual over the lifetime of the club. Along with Domenic, Subculture has also set the tone for the club from 1994 onwards.

How have Glasgow people had an impact on Sub Club?
The warmth of the people in Glasgow is legendary of course, and rightly so. With the atmosphere in the Sub Club when it's going full tilt it is the best club vibe of any I've witnessed – honorary mention to the Haçienda at its peak).

What Glasgow creative soul would you like the club to collaborate with?
David Byrne was born in Dumbarton which is almost Glasgow and he would

definitely top my list of inspirations from the West of Scotland.

If you could go for dinner with two famous Glaswegians, who would they be?
John Martyn and Billy Connolly.

Any tips for folk trying to run a small creative business in Glasgow?
Never give up on your dreams – roll with the punches and keep getting back on your feet.

What are your expectations of returning to the Sub Club every single Saturday at Harri & Domenic's Subculture?
The best house music night in the world in my opinion so no reason to think it will be any less when we reopen – I imagine the energy on the re-opening night will be pretty mind-blowing.

---

17 The Thornwood Bar
A traditional Partick pub that was recently given an upgrade. The Thornwood is considered one of Glasgow's first Art Deco pubs and the refurbishment was sympathetic to its heritage, retaining the original panelling, cornicing and wooden bar. This fun neighbourhood spot is run by Marc Ferrier, co-owner of the Admiral Bar on Waterloo Street, alongside business partner Kenny Hamilton. You'll get a soup and a sandwich, or go for their popular mac 'n' cheese with your pint.
📍 724 Dumbarton Road, G11 6RB 📞 0141 334 5059
🌐 thethornwoodbar.com

18 Tiki Bar & Kitsch Inn
A ray of sunshine on Bath Street. Say aloha to a basement bar with a big personality, take a seat on a peacock chair and sip on a tropical cocktail served in a ceramic tiki mug. They are serious about their drinks, but they have a sense of humour about everything else. They launched a Thai barbeque menu earlier this year and have expanded their outdoor area, somehow managing to lift in a customised Airstream bar to this sunken

enclave. A zombie cocktail is not for the faint-hearted.
📍 214 Bath Street, G2 4HW 📞 0141 332 1341
🌐 tikibarglasgow.com

19 Dukes Bar
Compact, unassuming and cool corner bar. They are near to the action in Finnieston but happy enough to do their own thing. Regular open mic night, when circumstances allow. The Clash played here in 1985 on their 'busking tour'. The tables are made from the running track of nearby Kelvin Hall. This year they have added outside seating, a coffee machine and sourdough toasties made by Kitchenetta in Hyndland. Check the gantry for their rum selection.
📍 41 Old Dumbarton Road, G3 8RD 📞 0141 339 7821
🌐 dukes-bar.co.uk

20 The Old Toll Bar
A piece of Kinning Park's history that was pushed into the present when owner Mido Soliman reinvented this Victorian saloon, retaining its classic interior while bringing together local musicians, DJs and comedians to add to the

roster of regular entertainment. One day you might be able to play your own vinyl records on the bar turntable, the next there might be a folk group playing in the corner.

Downstairs is decorated by Rogue One murals featuring Glasgow personalities. You can admire Kelly McDonald, Taggart actor Mark McManus, Sharleen Spiteri and Harri from Sub Club on the walls of the speakeasy lounge while enjoying a cocktail.
📍 1 Paisley Rd West, G51 1LF 📞 0141 258 4830
🌐 oldtollbarglasgow.com

Whisky City

GLASGOW HAS A LONG relationship with whisky. There may not be as many distilleries as there used to be across the city, but places like Chivas Brothers in the Gorbals maintain that link. In terms of bars, there's the great whisky cathedrals of The Bon Accord, The Pot Still, The Lismore and then pubs that have a long-established part to play in Glasgow's social life like The Horse Shoe Bar, The Scotia, The Clutha and The Ben Nevis. Each neighbourhood has somewhere you could go for a hawf and hawf – a half pint of beer and a wee nip to go with it. Glasgow's original improvised whisky cocktail.

Over the last decade, whisky has assumed a more prominent place in local hospitality, breaking free of preconceptions and finding a new appreciative audience. You'll find restaurants with well stocked whisky collections – Ubiquitous Chip and Two Fat Ladies at the Buttery would be good examples - but there's also Porter & Rye who serve some of the finest drinks in Finnieston, The Anchor Line with its beautifully appointed bar and more recently Glaschu which opened with a whisky cocktail menu inspired by the history of the city and a comfortable lounge overlooking Royal Exchange Square. In many ways, this gradual shift has been Glasgow catching up with the momentum of whisky internationally as the spirit is considered a key ingredient in mixed drinks outside of Scotland as much as it is something to be enjoyed in a glass with a drop of water.

Alex Robertson is the global head of heritage and education for The Glenlivet whisky, based in offices on Blythswood Square. He has visited more than 60 countries around the world talking about single malts. He says: "The biggest change I've seen has been the move towards cocktail culture. We're seeing Glasgow embrace that. You get an opportunity to explore the flavour of Scotch whisky in an accessible way. We don't have to be sitting on the sidelines discussing whether it should just be mixed with water or ice."

"We have an extensive cocktail menu with The Glenlivet now. We released a whisky called The Glenlivet Caribbean Reserve which lends itself to traditional Mai Tai cocktails. This is a new phase for whisky. I think it all fits in with modern Scottish hospitality."

In terms of developing different iterations of The Glenlivet, the original Speyside single malt, the cask the spirit is matured in can add different texture: "Every distillery follows the same process. It's three basic ingredients; malted barley, yeast, water and the distilling is all defined in law. You can point to where the differences occur. It could be the water source – the water for The Glenlivet has a high mineral content, which for Scotland is unusual. It's not like soft water in Glasgow. We have incredibly tall stills at the distillery, which leads to the delicate, smooth, balanced spirit that we're known for. Then there's what our Master Distiller Alan Winchester calls the "magic of location" – things like our supply of local barley. You simply can't make The Glenlivet anywhere else because it would taste different."

"Then finally, in the East End of Glasgow we make these barrels using American oak or European oak and we have been using Cognac casks or rum casks to influence the flavour. You have two things open to you as a distiller to change your whisky – age and cask.

Of course, you will still see whisky being enjoyed with a beer – "why not? A refreshing drink with a balanced spirit" – but Alex sees the next wave of local bars driving innovation: "Scotland is the home of whisky so there is a traditional approach but there's also an evolution of the bartender as a profession, someone who can create new expressions and it brings a good energy to the bars, encouraging more people to ask for new drinks. I think that's on the rise in Glasgow. The complexity of Scotch whisky like The Glenlivet is perfectly suited to a cocktail serve."

Top bars in the city have created cocktails to celebrate The Best of Glasgow. Order them on your next visit.

For more whisky recipes and local recommendations, visit ⊕ glasgowist.com/TheGlenlivet

Glaschu *"The Barr"*

A drink created in homage to the Barr family who created Scotland's 'other national drink'.

40ml The Glenlivet Founder's Reserve
15ml Grand Marnier
Bar spoon of apricot jam
20ml Lemon Juice
2 dashes of Orange Bitters
Egg white

Method Dry shake with egg white, then wet shake with ice. Fine strain and top with Barr's Cream Soda.

The Amsterdam *"Tiramisu"*

This is our indulgent end of the night dessert drink. We call it the Tiramisu in homage to the classic Italian dessert.

45ml The Glenlivet Founder's Reserve
7.5ml Gravino
10ml Tonka syrup
10ml Pandan
25ml Espresso (or strong cold brew)
15ml Cacao nib infused oloroso
12.5ml Nonino

10ml Cross Brew coffee liqueur
1 whole egg

Method Shake then serve in a Lotus biscuit crumbed glass and garnish with chocolate dust.

The Citizen
"Citizen's Advce"   "St Vincent"

The Citizen's take on a Rob Roy, using The Glenlivet Caribbean Reserve. This is a short drink served straight up.

We used a homemade chocolate and ginger infused vermouth to lift the sweet and tropical notes of this rum barrel aged selection.

50ml The Glenlivet Caribbean Reserve
25ml Chocolate and Ginger infused Cocchi di Torino
1 dash of chocolate bitters

Method Stirred down over ice and served neat in a Nick & Nora glass with a grated dark chocolate rim.

This will be The Citizen's signature whisky highball to mark the Best of Glasgow. It's a long drink using The Glenlivet Founder's Reserve.

We used a homemade hibiscus infused vermouth, calvados, and pink grapefruit liqueur to create a refreshing highball drink that compliments the smooth and balanced notes of the Founder's Reserve.

35ml The Glenlivet Founder's Reserve
15ml Hibiscus infused Cocchi Americano
15ml Pink Grapefrut Liqueur
10ml Calvados

Method Built in a sling glass over cubed ice, topped up with tonic water and stirred. Garnished with a slice of pink grapefruit and a sprig of mint.

The Gate *"The Smuggler"*

The bar team at The Gate create a new cocktail list every six weeks and enjoy working with interesting whiskies to create new flavour combinations. To celebrate the Best of Glasgow they worked together to create The Smuggler which you can order on your next visit.

50ml The Glenlivet Caribbean Reserve
10ml Amarosa Rosehip Liqueur
15ml Granny Smith Apple Cordial
5ml Maple syrup

Method Stirred down, over a block, garnished with an apple slice.

BEST OF GLASGOW

Your guide to people and places across the city

Football adjacent nature reserve
THE CLAYPITS
📍 beside Firhill Stadium, G20 7AL

The Claypits Local Nature Reserve sits beside the Forth and Clyde Canal. It's linked with the National Walking Cycling Network and thanks to recent funding now features an all-weather path to explore 25 acres of woodland and wetland, about a mile from the city centre. Local wildlife include herds of roe deer. You'll also find spectacular views across the city. On a clear day, you can see the Isle of Arran in the distance. A new Garscube Bridge across the canal links the nature reserve to Firhill Stadium.

Ancient trees
FOSSIL GROVE
📍 Victoria Park, G14 9QR

In late 1887, a path was cut as part of the new Victoria Park. It uncovered the first of eleven fossil tree stumps from the Carboniferous Period. They are about 330 million years old and preserved where the grew. The Fossil Grove Trust work with the Council to present and preserve the fossils in the building that was erected over the earth heritage site.

Boat builders
GALGAEL
📍 15 Fairley Street, G51 2SN 📞 0141 427 3070
🌐 *galgael.org*

The sign outside says "GalGael Est. 9th Century". Govan has a long and storied relationship with the River Clyde. These days, there's only two shipyards left, and the channels of the Clyde are mostly undisturbed by vessels. GalGael Trust was founded in the mid-1990s by Colin Macleod.

It is a community and heritage association that builds and sails wooden boats as a way of preserving ancient local skills. It provides a cultural anchor point by offering practical activities and a sense of purpose. The space is also a safe harbour for those whose lives have been battered by storms such as unemployment, depression or addiction. Plans for the future include digital workshops and remote learning. Buying their products or making use of their services contributes to the valuable work they continue to do in the community. There's a range of crafted products available at their online shop.

Allotment
GREYFRIARS GARDEN
📍 Nicholas Street, G1 1QB
🅕 greyfriarsgarden

Hidden in plain sight, Greyfriars Garden is a tranquil space in the Merchant City - a modern growing garden on a medieval site. Home to raised beds, greenhouses, a small wildflower meadow and picnic tables. Greyfriars Garden Association, drawn from residents of Drygate, Merchant City and Trongate areas have access. The adjacent Deanside Well Medieval Garden is a public space featuring well stones that date back to a 15th century Franciscan friary that occupied this site.

Art Deco dining room
ROGANO
📍 11 Exchange Place, G1 3AN 📞 0141 248 4055
🌐 roganoglasgow.com

Experience the time-capsule effect of escaping the busy streets around Buchanan Street, to be enveloped by the Art Deco style that was set when Rogano opened in 1935. Back then, the Cunard liner Queen Mary was being built on the Clyde, and that became the defining design influence. The restaurant retains an element of stardust from a bygone era.

Elizabeth Taylor, Bob Dylan and Rod Stewart are among the luminaries who have dined here. Benedict Cumberbatch filmed here and stayed on for martinis. The restaurant will reopen in 2021.

Fore Play Crazy Golf

Crazy Golf
FORE PLAY CRAZY GOLF
📍 124 Portman Street G41 1EJ
🌐 foreplaycrazygolf.co.uk

This Kinning Park venue features a crazy golf course populated by mini versions of local landmarks, including the Finnieston Crane. They've developed close relationships with local craft beer and street food operators to create an evolving roster of food and drink options while also providing a stage for local artists.

Magic shop
TAM SHEPHERDS
📍 33 Queen Street, G1 3EF
🌐 tamshepherds.com

The exterior of Tam Shepherds looks like it's got no business being in the centre of the third biggest city in Britain in the year 2021. Yet business it does. Healthy business. This unassuming 'trick shop' that's been going

since 1886. It sells all manner of hats, masks and fancy dress garb - but the real magic lies in the range of props and books on illusions built up over generations. A curious little nugget of delight, mere metres from the department stores of Argyle Street.

Steamboat
PS WAVERLEY
📍 50 Pacific Quay, G51 1EA
🌐 waverleyexcursions.co.uk

Lobbying from the Temperance Movement, started by John Dunlop in Glasgow in 1829, led to an act of parliament aimed at curbing local drinking habits. As a result, pubs were shut after 11pm at night and the sale of alcohol in Scotland's public houses was banned on a Sunday. The prohibition didn't apply to those travelling on passenger boats.

So, on a Sunday, steamboat companies would compete on the Broomielaw, charging a small fee to take passengers down the Clyde to destinations like Rothesay, Dunoon and Gourock, serving drinks on the way. The legal loophole created the world's first booze cruise, and the word "steaming" entered local usage.

PS Waverley, was the last paddle boat built in Glasgow in 1946 and is the last sea-faring passenger-carrying paddle boat that still runs anywhere in the world today. After a recent restoration of its engines, trips are set to continue for many summers to come. The boat is moored beside the Glasgow Science Centre.

In 1974, Billy Connolly played a banjo onboard, singing a song he wrote called Clydescope: "Grab a steamer and sail down the Clyde. No kidding, it's a magic way to spend a day. Try it on The Waverley".

Pub art

📍 Ashton Lane and Byres Road

You can drink alongside Alasdair Gray's artwork in three different parts of Ubiquitous Chip. The most famous piece is the mural on the staircase that takes you downstairs

from The Brasserie to The Wee Pub. Many faces on the wall belong to staff and friends, including original restaurant owner Ronnie Clydeside. The paintings were completed around the time The Chip first opened, with Gray painting the murals in return for food and drink.

At Òran Mór, formerly the Kelvinside Parish Church, Gray's mural *(above)* is

one of the largest pieces of public art in Scotland. Painted along the ceiling of the auditorium in a wonderful blue, the work depicts figures of local legend, with hidden meaning and symbols built in. Gray is most famously known for his novel Lanark, which was written over a period of 30 years.

Dubbed the father figure of the renaissance of Scottish literature and art by The Guardian, his work combines the fantastic and the mundane, with many of his portraits featuring characters in his stories.

Climbing wall cafe
GLASGOW CLIMBING CENTRE
📍 534 Paisley Rd W, G51 1RN 📞 0141 427 9550
🌐 *glasgowclimbingcentre.com*

Reach new heights when you master the skills to conquer the vertical walls and steep overhangs at this nationally accredited centre. Build up an appetite across routes that rise up to 16 metres high. When you

Sign of the times

CIARÁN GLÖBEL is an artist and graphic designer who uses traditional sign-writing tools and techniques to produce striking, hand-painted work that's become a feature on the the the high street and helped define the identity of emerging local businesses. You can see his signs at the likes of Potbelly, Phillies of Shawlands, KAF, Argyle St Arches and Bag O'Nails.

When you see your signs at places that have become very recognisable parts of Glasgow, is that something that makes you proud?
I like the idea of having a legacy left behind. I'm under no illusion that every wee coffee shop or bar I go and paint will be open for years. But there are places that will outlive me.

I come from a graffiti background and I used to write a nom de guerre - a name up on a wall - and that would be my legacy. I would pass by that wall every week, see that it was still there and my mark had been made. You hit adulthood and realise that you have responsibilities. I found that signwriting was a way to leave my mark, get paid and not face any repercussions. Now I get lots of kindness instead of being chased away.

How has signwriting become valued again in Glasgow?
It's connected to the emergence of the street food scene a few years ago. Street food has only been a word in our lexicon for the last five years. I never thought of street food when I was a teenager. So, when this whole thing happened, it was driven by younger

people who were closer to folk that had studied graphic design or were painters so they were brought in to create the look of their food brand. Instagram ran alongside all that so people recognised the work and knew where to find me and others. Then when street food and pop-up operators started opening their own shops, the artwork would be an important part of that.

Is there a lot of crossover, then, between the people involved in art and food and music in Glasgow?
I worked at Argyle St Arches when it became Platform and I recognised lots of people I met there. They were ex-art students or they used to be in a band, you can chat about ideas. I think being able to find people to work with makes you realise that we're pretty good at doing our own thing and going our own way in Glasgow. Why not? All you need to do is look at a list of artists or bands that this city has produced and that's your answer.
📷 *ciaranglobel*

Electric Dreams

ILLYUS & BARRIENTOS Ivan Hall Barrientos has Chilean parents and was born in America, while Illyus Brown grew up in Frankfurt after being born in Govan. They met on Glasgow's dance floors in 2014, building a friendship over their mutual love of modern house music. While Illyus was growing up in the local hip-hop scene in Germany, then distributing early mixtapes to pals in Glasgow, Barrientos was taking classical piano lessons. In the studio, these different influences combined to produce what has become the electronic duo's sound.

Where is your favourite place to eat in Glasgow?
There's a little vegetarian gem in the Southside called Ranjit's Kitchen. We're not vegetarians at all but there's something about a simple, flavoursome afternoon curry that hits the spot.

Where would you take your best pal for a pint?
We love The Belle on Great Western Road or Ubiquitous Chip. Pints and fireplaces in both are a must for us.

What's been the biggest Glasgow influence on your music?
Probably The Arches to be honest. Nights like Death Disco influenced Glasgow in many ways, one of them being the music of course. But it also created an amazing culture within the clubbing community.

Was becoming a DJ then music producer always the plan?
Illyus: I come from a hip hop background which is totally different from Barrientos'. I moved into the DJ world when I was around 18 and eventually thought to myself "how can I expand this journey of mine." That naturally took me into producing music.
Barrientos: As Illyus mentioned our stories when it comes to music are quite different. I'm classically trained and have been part of an orchestral environment. But I've always been a huge fan of electronic music so my progression into producing came from being a fan first and foremost. The DJ part came later.

What's your favourite Glasgow saying?
Our mate Kieran always says "wan wae the heid and wan wae the bunnet". To this day we still don't know what he's on about...
ⓘ illyusandbarrientos

---

make it back down, Liam Mcalpine runs the Balcony Cafe at the centre and has a great reputation for quirky and interesting recipes. His Flavabomb Project Kitchen hosts pop-up dinner events.

Park bench
THE KNITTED BENCH
◉ Botanic Gardens, G12 OUE

Rita McGurn was a designer for film and television, an artist and an enthusiastic knitter, creating sculptures in wool. When Rita died, her daughter Mercedes was sitting on their

favourite bench when she had the idea of creating an installation in tribute.

After help from family and friends, the bench was covered in a patchwork of bright colours and small knitted birds. The bench sits in the gardens from March until the end of September.

City cinemas
EVERYMAN CINEMA
◉ Princes Square, G1 3JN
🌐 *everymancinema.com/glasgow*

Glasgow is a cinema city. Enthusiasm for going to the pictures is an enduring feature of local social life. Cineworld on Renfrew Street is the world's tallest cinema. There's an IMAX at the Glasgow Science Centre. The Odeon at Glasgow Quay was one of the first of the chain's properties in the UK to be upgraded to Luxe status with reclining chairs, making it the comfiest cinema in the city. Meanwhile, the GFT is the home of the

Glasgow Film Festival and a showcase for new and classic films throughout the year. For the best cinema in the city right now, look to Everyman which provides a comfortable experience for all the family in a quirky, small space within Princes Square.

Street Food

TRUSTY BUCK'S They were a new vegan food truck business preparing for a busy summer of events when lockdown began. With no crowds to cater for, Hugh Kearns changed his plans and created a home delivery operation working out of the driveway of his parents' home in Pollokshields while employing out of work musician pals as couriers.

This food story begins with Hugh working as a manager for BrewDog while performing as Trusty Buck Arlington, his washboard-playing country music alter-ego, every Saturday in McSorley's. Deciding that he wanted to launch his own vegan menu and get on the road, he spent last year refurbishing a horsebox, converting it into a quirky mobile space for preparing curries, burritos and fries.

With the launch of the business stalled and events cancelled, Hugh moved in a different direction. "It was obvious what I needed to do. I was in a lucky situation because we had started a kitchen residency in the Linen 1906 pub, so we had the beginnings of a customer base in the Southside. There was space in my parent's driveway, where the food truck was already being stored. We set up a gazebo in the garden, brought in pallets to set up a floor, and moved the whole operation into the driveway. That was my kitchen – we tried to keep on top of the swearing, for the neighbours." Environmental health officers were able to help authorise the operation and Trusty Buck's received plenty of local support.

The vegetarian haggis burritos with Buckfast caramelised carrot that have been flying out of a Southside driveway kitchen alongside vegetarian munchie boxes will soon be available from a new delivery unit in Dalmarnock.
⊕ *trustybucks.co.uk*

Our other favourites...

MOSTAR MUNCH Tasty sausage kebabs from the Balkans, spiced with paprika and garlic, served in a warmed flatbread with sauce and salad. Find them at Big Feed in a reworked warehouse space in Govan.
⊕ *big-feed.com/mostar-balkan-kebabs*

SHAWARMARAMA Bright and spicy Middle Eastern flavoured delights. Find them outdoors at SWG3, or order a delivery to your door from their kitchen in The Gorbals.
🅕 *shawarmararocks*

SALT 'N' CHILLI A menu that was made for Glasgow. Tofu, chicken, chips all with an added kick. One of Big Feed's most popular street food traders. When festivals are back, they'll be there.
⊕ *big-feed.com/salt-n-chilli*

GRANNY BEATON'S Normally found at the Partick Food Market where you can pick up Empire biscuits, Ecclefechan tart, clootie dumpling and tattie scones. You can also organise deliveries of homemade soup to your door online.
⊕ *grannybeatons.co.uk*

Hidden coffee place
OTTOMAN COFFEEHOUSE
📍 73 Berkeley Street, G3 7DX,
⊕ *ottomancoffeehouse.co.uk*

Imran Akhtar is the co-owner of the Ottoman Coffee House, along with his brother Irfan. Their father originally bought this space intending it to be a restaurant. It sits behind the former Glasgow Society for Musicians and what was the Shah Noor Indian restaurant on Berkeley Street.

A beautiful room with high ceilings, comfy sofas, chess sets, furnishings bought from the Grand Bazaar in Istanbul, portraits of Sultans. After being used for private functions it has emerged as a community coffeehouse serving Yemani coffee and some food items. They run a kitchen to help those in need, providing food packages to the homeless.

Their mission statement: "Our ambition is to establish the bridges between the nostalgic coffeehouse of the Ottoman past and the present, operating as both a café and a meditation space in the heart of the West End of Glasgow, the perfect location for morning coffee, afternoon tea, reading the papers and catching your breath".

Bus journey
CITY SIGHTSEEING TOUR
⊕ *citysightseeingglasgow.co.uk*

Find your seat on the top deck and glide around city streets with a clear view of local landmarks. Your tour guide will keep you entertained as you move through the east and west of the city. Even if you think you've seen it all, you'll pick up a new local perspective.

Sweetie shop
GLICKMAN'S
📍 157 London Rd, Glasgow G1 5BX 📞 0141 552 0880
⊕ *glickmans.co.uk*

Glickman's, established in 1903, is the oldest sweetie shop in Glasgow where nostalgia nestles in every jar of soor plooms. Jamie Oliver visited to watch them make macaroon cake in traditional copper pots. Their shop on London Road is stocked with the colourful treats of your childhood.

Join the Glasgow mural trail to see some of the works brightening up city streets as walls become canvases for a new generation of artists.

ART AND CREATIVE expression were at the heart of Glasgow's cityscape, but at some point we lost our way a bit and there were times in recent decades when parts of the city looked just like anywhere else. That familiar local sense of individuality was lacking. Then there were the invisible edges of the city centre, the lanes or streets where people walked by studying their feet, forgetting to acknowledge what's around them.

A conscious effort to add more character and brighten up buildings began in 2008 and is an ongoing endeavour. Even if you think you

Artists can apply to a city council mural fund if they have an idea for new street art. Art Pistol, Rogue-One and Smug have become key players in elevating Glasgow's street art scene. Gaz Mac has created a focus for the community out of the SWG3 complex of arts venues - they host Yardworks, an international festival of graffiti and design, while providing studio

Street Art
makes Glasgow

have spotted all these street canvases, there will be moments when you find yourself stopped in your tracks looking again at a floating taxi or an urban nature scene bursting out of a gable end or folk playing badminton suspended above cobbled streets.

We occasionally find ourselves waving to the image of Billy Connolly beside the Hootenanny pub after a few pints. The High Street murals of St Mungo and St Enoch are a source of community pride.

Clockwise from left: Rebel Bear's NHS art work on Ashton Lane, Mark Worst's Thenue on Abercromby Street, Star Wars' Boba Fett at Yardworks Glasgow

space for new artists.

This year, Rebel Bear was responsible for pandemic related pieces that added commentary and encouragement. He also created an artwork celebrating the NHS on Ashton Lane while Cobolt Collective, the all-female mural art team celebrated key workers in a typography and illustrations campaign.

There's a City Centre Mural Trail to guide you around the more prominent artworks that have become emblematic of Glasgow.
⊕ *citycentremuraltrail.co.uk*

GORDON TERRIS

My Glasgow

ALEX KAPRANOS

Songwriter, lead singer with Franz Ferdinand

GLASGOW HAS SO MUCH going for it. If I have friends over from a foreign country, like USA or France, I will always take them on a tour to show the place off. Go for a pint, take them for something good to eat and then a trip to the transport museum so they can have a look at my old Lambretta scooter.

It's difficult to choose my favourite Glasgow building, as there is so much magnificent architecture in the city. It used to be the Newbery Tower at the Glasgow School Of Art, but they pulled it down because Brutalist Architecture fell out of fashion. It's such a shame.

My favourite outdoors space is The Necropolis after a snowfall. It's magical. We've got so many restaurants too. I'm not really up on what restaurants are cool. I was away on tour for three years, then came back to a lockdown. I like 111 by Modou and Mother India will always be a favourite.

I'd say the best pub is The Laurieston on Bridge Street and I like going to Mono too. I can't drink coffee because it tastes so disgusting, but I'm sure you can get a tasty vegan cup there. I love the vibe of that place. Good people.

I go clothes shopping in TK Maxx. It's great. You can really get a bargain. The one on Argyle Street is better than the Sauchiehall Street one, though.

Glasgow has got great music. The problem is that there are too many to mention. That's one of those good kinds of problems. It would start with Orange Juice, via Primal Scream, The Jesus and Mary Chain, the Bellshill boys (Teenage Fanclub, BMX Bandits) through all those bands of the Kazoo Club era in the 90s who were so important to me, like Urusei Yatsura, Bis, Stanleys, Yummy Fur, Eska, Tarot Marrow, Trout, Glen Or Glenda, Savilles, Pink Kross, Lisa Helps The Blind, Lungleg, Mogwai, Me Hubby and Tom, through to bands that came after like Late Night Foreign Radio, The Royal We, Remember Remember, Mother and The Addicts to the bands that are doing some exciting things at the moment, like Walt Disco, Vegan Leather and Medicine Cabinet.

I moved to Dennistoun in 2000. I like the vibe and, in recent years, exciting wee places have opened up. I'm just sad that the tailor and the cobbler by Duke Street shut down.

My Glasgow hero is Alasdair Gray. The deepest inspiration in so many fields. What a great mind and a true artist for an entire lifetime. He changed the way I love the city.

Local hero, the late Alasdair Gray

JULIE HOWDEN

River City

Glasgow made the Clyde, and the Clyde made Glasgow. Singapore photographer Andy Yong captured this image of the river meandering through the city while studying here. It's published here for the first time. ⊕ andyyongphoto.com

the New Creatives

Writer **Madeleine Dunne** speaks to some of the young team contributing to the life of the city.

AMY MATTHEWS
Comedian

Hailing from Essex, Amy is a stand-up comedian, host, presenter and writer based in Glasgow. Amy has called Scotland home since 2017, and in that time has made waves on the comedy circuit. Hotly tipped for future success, Amy took home the Best Newcomer accolade at the 2019 Scottish Comedy Awards.

Her first adult comedy zine, 'NEBULA', was published in October. "I've been doing comedy for three years and started in Scotland, so the Scottish comedy circuit is most certainly home for me. I've had some of my favourite gigs ever at The Stand in Glasgow. I miss it so much and cannot wait to be back.

Lockdown has seen a pause on live comedy as we know it, but I've been pleasantly surprised at the innovation and new avenues comic creativity has found during this time. I've done a few drive-in gigs throughout the pandemic, and online gigs, too.

"Glasgow is a city that has a misjudged reputation from onlookers outside of it, an entirely different reputation among the people who actually live here, and a deep-rooted sense of identity that's intrinsic to and symbiotic with its inhabitants – as someone from Essex, I think I can identify pretty well with that summary.

"I moved here during lockdown into a top floor

flat without a garden, so I had to sniff out the greenspace pretty sharpish. The Botanics, the walk along the banks of the River Kelvin and Kelvingrove Park very quickly became my favourite places in Glasgow; perhaps because of their association, for me, with the hour of freedom and fresh air a day during peak lockdown, but also because they're objectively beautiful. The bridges and underpasses along the Kelvin have an oddly Studio Ghibli style aesthetic magic to them, and the Arboretum and Herb Garden in the Botanics make you feel miles away from the city."
🌐 *amymatthewscomedy.com*

PAUL BLACK
Writer

Paul Black is a writer, director, and performer from the Southside of Glasgow. Perhaps best known for his viral comedy sketches on social media, including one of a vlogger giving a hilarious tour of Glasgow through the eyes of an American, Paul continues to expertly capture the warmth and humour of Glasgow's denizens as his career in film and TV progresses.

"I have been making short films since I was young, but decent looking films are difficult to make with no money, so I started out posting comedy sketches on Twitter and Facebook filmed with a crew of my friends and family. After these got a few views I was able to start making comedy content for BBC Scotland, starting with their Short Stuff platform and most recently I was able to write and direct a sketch show comedy special with them. In between writing gigs, I work freelance as a runner on productions.

"One thing I like about Glasgow – that I think also works to its detriment – is the way in which we slag each other. I think it's quite easy to work in comedy when a lot of the people around you are naturally funny, the slaggings that are ingrained in our culture have given us all a bit of a thicker skin and allows you to see the humour in everything. That being said, it definitely holds us back in the creative industry. Everybody's scared to try something in case they get slagged, so who knows, maybe it's a bad thing!

I love the GFT. I remember going there when I was 14 and instantly gaining a superiority complex over my Odeon-attending peers. There's loads of other places I love, like Pollok Park, I grew up just beside it and spent a lot of time there."
🌐 *brennanartists.com/clients/ paul-black*

JOSEPH EPEMOLU
Amplify Black Voices

Born and raised in the Greater Glasgow Area, Joseph Epemolu is a recent product design graduate, photographer and all-round creative. During lockdown he launched Amplify Black Voices, a clothing brand that donates all profits to charities that support the Black Lives Matter movement.

"I recently graduated from Edinburgh Napier University in Product Design after submitting my major project of making denim for disability while developing my skillsets across design, fashion and photography. In lockdown, I have created my own clothing brand and store called Amplify Black Voices which donates 100 per cent of its profits to different charities that advocate for the prosperity and protection of POC from systemic racism.

"I love Glasgow because it's very down to earth and resilient. I feel like Glasgow is used to playing second string to Edinburgh, but it knows with a confidence that it's a fantastic city. It can be rough around the edges, but the people of Glasgow are some of the friendliest, open and accepting people I've had the pleasure of meeting, even with the unsavoury displays

@JAE_MEDIA

of racism and intolerance that can be shown. The people really do make Glasgow. As long as people are willing to work hard and show grit and determination then Glasgow accepts you for the most part.

I personally love Barrowlands, The Lighthouse and the Kelvingrove and Botanic Garden area. Glasgow provides a lot of opportunities to learn, grow and expand your way of thinking and no matter how much time I spend here, there is always a capacity to learn or see something new."
🌐 *amplifyblackvoices.co.uk*

Ruth Leiser

ROOBS
GRLCLB

Ruth Leiser is the founder of GRLCLB, and a post-grad psychology student. GRLCLB is a Glasgow-born and based brand that prides itself on being everything that Amazon's not; ethically-sourced and locally-printed pieces that are size-inclusive, gender neutral, and designed, wrapped and shipped by one person. Ruth also uses her platform online to talk about mental health and educate people in a jargon-free, accessible way.

"I was born and raised in the Southside of Glasgow, so its biggest draw for me is that it's home. I truly believe it's one of those places that 'just has something about it' – I can never put my finger on why it's so special, or what makes it different to everywhere else, but there's a joyous sense of camaraderie involved in calling this place your home. I've never been anywhere else that has such a sense of self-deprecation, and simultaneously pride.

My favourite places in Glasgow are the ones I always forget about until I'm either back there,

or far from here and hit by a pang of homesickness. Just thinking about the Barrowland Ballroom makes me want to cry. I love Pollok Park because it reminds me of being wee. I'm probably not alone in being convinced the shop near my mum and dad's does the best ice-cream in the world. I remember the hill at my secondary school's ash pitch where we went sledging and someone went flying right through the fence. I miss the ABC more than I can put into words and can't comprehend that all these future generations of teenagers won't get to scream along to *I Bet You Look Good On The Dancefloor* while clutching a VK Blue. Take me just about anywhere in this city and there'll be a memory; good or bad or drunk or bent-over-laughing-hilarious".
🌐 *grlclb.com*

LEYLA JOSEPHINE
Writer and performer

Leyla Josephine is a writer and performer from Glasgow, best known for her performance poetry. She has made two autobiographical theatre shows to date and is currently writing and directing her first short film, Groom.

"I'm a writer and performer, but I run a lot of workshops alongside my own practice and work in different social contexts facilitating others to be creative. It sounds a bit all over the place, but all my different roles and projects really inform each other.

I love the familiarity of Glasgow. I like knowing my way around, seeing people that I've known for years when I'm out and about. I love the food, the bars, the good chat, meeting strangers in the smoking areas, the parties. There's a weird rule in Glasgow that if you're in the car no matter where you are, you're never further than 20 minutes from another place. I like how close it is to the country and if you get up high enough you can see always see the hills and mountains.

I love Kelvingrove Park, I've had so many good times there, from sledging as a child, sitting by the skate park when I was a teenager drinking cherry Lambrini, the royal wedding riot, lots of kissing and breakups, swimming in the river (wouldn't recommend), seeing Chic at the bandstand. Now, I love watching all the young people doing the same as I did, getting into trouble, living obliviously fun lives. I go there now to catch up with a friend or take the dog down Kelvin walkway – much more civilised. I love that park, how the seasons change it and how many memories I have made there."
🌐 *leylajosephine.co.uk*

MARIA SLEDMERE & DENISE BONETTI
SPAM Zine

Maria Sledmere and Denise Bonetti are the editor-in-chief and founding/managing editor of SPAM Press, an indie poetry press which started in Glasgow in 2016 and now operates between Glasgow, London and Berlin.

SPAM publishes books, pamphlets, zines, anthologies and an online poetry magazine. They run a podcast (URL Sonata), a lively reviews space (SPAM Plaza) and host regular readings, parties and other events.

MS: "Our semi-serious slogan is 'MAKE POETRY COOL AGAIN' and we describe ourselves as post-internet. The idea is to make space for poetry that feeds into our hypermediated moment while

JORDAN LATIMER
Partycat Clothing

Jordan Latimer is an independent fashion designer originally hailing from Belfast, but a Glasgow native for the last three years. She handmakes clothes and accessories with a focus on embodying her own "High Femme Camp aesthetic", while also being as ethical, sustain-

also challenging what counts as poetry – memes, toilet graffiti, YouTube comments, TripAdvisor reviews and lyric remixes might be included.

DB: "Maebh Harper and I started SPAM about 5 years ago not really having a clue what we were doing, and not knowing if anyone would be as keen as we were to see what a magazine for poetry rooted in internet culture would look like. It's really nice to see what a long way we've come, and so wholesome to see people respond so positively to our projects.

MS: I've been here for nine years (I grew up in Ayrshire) and can't quite seem to get away. It's the perfect size for maintaining a lively DIY scene, not to mention the hospitable venues that have supported our launches and pub-

able and inclusive as possible.

"It's important to me that my clothes help represent queer people like me, and I also want my clothes to be accessible and available to any size of person or bank account. I don't think personal expression or ethics should only be for thin people and I also don't think it should be behind massive paywalls.

Being from Belfast, one of my favourite things about Glasgow is how similar it feels to home, just a lot bigger. I also love the queer scene here, it's very friendly and inclusive and I've ended up making most of my best friends through having that in common and being in that community. I've also got a good client base with some of the local drag queens, who always have fun custom orders and make my work look stunning.

My bit is in Rutherglen, I love my little flat and I love all the charity shops around me that I can find the best random accesso-

ries and pieces for photoshoots or inspiration in. The Barra's market is a good one too, and the fabric bazaar there is my favourite go to fabric shop for stuff I don't need to order online."

🌐 *partycatclothing.bigcartel.com*

SAMAR ZIADAT
Founder & Director,
Dardishi Festival

Samar Ziadat is an activist, independent curator, researcher, and editor. She has worked in programming and coordinating roles at the Scottish Queer International Film Festival (SQIFF) and the Glasgow Zine Library, as well as delivering her own courses and workshops on self-publishing and intersectional feminism. Her contributions have been recognised as part of the Young Women's Movement Scotland's 30 under 30 list. She was shortlisted for the Arab British Centre Award for Culture 2019.

In 2016 Samar founded Dardishi, a community focused annual

zine and arts festival that showcases the cultural production of Arab and North African womxn in Glasgow. Dardishi also run year-round events designed to build and sustain community outside the Festival period.

"I've moved cities nine times in my life and so far, Glasgow is my favourite place. It's hard for me to say exactly why, but I know it has to do with the attitude of the

lications over the years. Glasgow has long had a strong spoken word scene and we started SPAM to supplement that with more experimental poetry. We want to support poems about Derrida, glitches and the end of capitalism as much as odes to chips and cheese.

Maria and Denise

DB: I grew up in Italy, and only moved to Glasgow at 19 to go to university. All the things I would want to say about the place reek of cliché: vibrant, friendly, accessible, creative, chaotic good. The problem is that it's all true. It's quite scary how quickly I have started thinking of it as home.

MS: In lockdown I've been exploring

the various necropolises of the city like the goth that I am, and mostly missing the poetry readings you'd normally find in hotspots like the CCA, Good Press and The Poetry Club. As a music journalist, the music scene here has always had a place in my heart, and venues like Mono, Stereo, Nice N Sleazy (which also hosts the brilliant spoken word/perfor-

mance/drag night *Queer Theory*), The Hug and Pint, Broadcast, The Flying Duck, The 13th Note and so on are super important in supporting DIY events.
DB: SPAM definitely owes its existence to the now-defunct gallery Voidoid Archive, run by Jason MacPhail. Jason kick-started the whole project not only by offering financial support for our first print run, but especially by being the first person beyond Maebh and I to believe in the project.

We also owe Jason our partnership with The Poetry Club, which allowed us to use the venue for our messy launch parties through the years. I don't think any other Glasgow venue could have been a better match for the kind of DIY odd/cheesy thing we were doing. And a huge shout out to the inimitable Good Press – a pillar of the arts community in Glasgow as well as a damn fine artist-run bookshop."

🌐 *spamzine.co.uk*

people who live here.

"Being in urban spaces is really central to my wellbeing, because, as a marginalised person, it's important for me to build community. However, it's actually all of the green spaces in this city that are most important and powerful to me."

🌐 *dardishi.com*

PHOEBE WILLISON
Design Weans

Phoebe Willison is a graphic designer and facilitator of creative events in Glasgow under the guise of Design Weans, a local organisation supporting emerging graphic designers and students making their way into the design industry.

Set up in 2017, Design Weans runs workshops, talks, networking evenings and exhibitions for Glasgow's creatives. They recently released a book and exhibition, Show Off and Show Up, showcasing the work of 102 visual communication graduates from nine institutions across Scotland whose degree shows were cancelled by the pandemic.

"Glasgow is my favourite place in the world. I was born here and went to school here, but I left to go to university in London and stayed there for almost seven years in the end, which was great and really invaluable. I moved back in 2017 and I never want to leave again.

I feel like it's a city of contradictions, the perfect blend of so welcoming but full of cheek, the weather's so wet and miserable but it doesn't stop everyone from being constantly up for having fun, even visually it's a bit of an industrial grey city, but the number of parks, and the fact you can so easily get out to the hills, balances it out.

Culturally and in terms of what we do as Design Weans, it's also great. We keep our events as accessible as possible, and if we charge

a ticket fee it's usually only £2-3, which means we often don't have much budget. We've found that on the whole people are really helpful, whether that's letting us hire a space for free, throwing in a few drinks for our attendees, or giving up time to share their skills.

While I do love the city and all of its buildings and people, my favourite places in Glasgow are green places, especially with a view. Like the flagpole in Queen's Park, or the viewpoint in Cathkin Braes, or the Necropolis. I also love places which feel like you're not even in the city, like along the Kelvin Way towards Maryhill. It's nice to get a wee bit of peace and being in these places always gives me perspective."

📷 *thedesignweans*

KATE MAXWELL
Curate. Glasgow

Kate Maxwell is the founder of Curate., an online directory for Glasgow creatives. Curate. aims to act as a discovery platform for independent artists, shops and creatives. It's set to be officially launched in November – just in time for Christmas.

"I work as a consultant for a global engineering firm where I specialise in logistics and waste management. Nothing that sexy! I've always had creative hobbies but never dedicated my time to honing a craft. I love unique pieces. Hand crafted local produce is often more sustainable, supports the local economy and creates an incredible type of community – I hope to harness this through Curate., and link both creatives and buyers and artists to artists. I want to create a space for beautiful crafts, arts and independent shops to be shared and

promoted and a central location for Glasgow locals to browse and explore local creatives.

"Glasgow has always felt like home to me because it's a lot like Manchester – architecturally, physically, spiritually. There is an easy, accessible community feel that I really missed when I was living in London – A seven-year stint really had me forgetting that people said hello to you in the shops. My partner is from Aberdeen but came to university in Glasgow, so we spent quite a lot of time up here before I moved.

I love a walk through Linn Park on a cold day, vegan bakes from Big Bear Bakery and the sourdough from Deanston Bakery. The Wuhan hot and dry noodles from Dumpling Monkey and a marinara from Paesano are two of my favourite things to eat and obviously, I'd drink a pint of Tennent's anywhere."

🌐 *curateglasgow.com*

My Glasgow

PAT KANE

Musician, journalist, and lead singer of Hue & Cry

AS ONE HALF OF POP DUO Hue & Cry, Pat Kane has performed on some of the city's greatest stages. A writer and political activist, we spoke to him about his personal perspective on the city.

What are your early memories of Glasgow?
Being taken into Goldberg's department store, doing Christmas shopping with my mum.

Were there books or music or other things that helped you form your first impressions of the city?
I used to laugh with my dad at Stanley Baxter's *Parliamo Glasgow*. I thought the place would be full of funny, quirky people.

How much would you say Glasgow is a character in your own music?
Quite explicitly in places – *Looking for Linda* begins in Glasgow Central.

And it's been our privilege to sing the late, great Micheal Marra's *Mother Glasgow* song for the last 30 years.

An anthem that's also critical of the city.

Are there parts of Glasgow you have a particular connection with?
I have recently fallen in love with the Cathedral district and the Necropolis – it reminds you of the imperial power and history of Glasgow, sometimes troublingly.

I am always going be hanging around North Glasgow – Hillhead, Partick, Maryhill. My university and music days were spent there.

Who are your Glasgow heroes?
Jimmy Reid, the firebrand socialist and supporter of independence, and my fellow Rector at Glasgow University. Billy Connolly, always, for his life journey. Also James Kelman, Scotland's best shot at a Nobel Prize for literature.

What local places would you recommend as the Best of Glasgow?
The CCA gift shop has saved my forgetful ass on many an occasion. Cafe Gandolfi is still the most boho-elegant, quirky place to meet and eat.

Favourite Glasgow venues?
I like The Hug and Pint – my daughter Eleanor Kane often gigs there.

If you are meeting folk around town, what do you like to do?
A coffee in Tinderbox Ingram Street is the best starting point. Then a wander round the city centre, from the raggedy to the glitzy end.

Do you have any favourite Glasgow buildings or views?
I recently stood just outside the new Transport Museum and looked down the River Clyde, with the Campsie hills beyond, and got a powerful sense of the trading and global history of Glasgow.

How would you describe Glasgow to someone who has never been here before?
I usually say that it's strung between "Glasvegas" (the indie band) and "Clydegrad" (Edwin Morgan's poem). Then they use Google to figure out what I'm talking about...

Pat Kane and his local hero Stanley Baxter (left)

The city is a patchwork of villages and high streets, each with their own personality and charms. Every community has its own story to tell. Take a wander through some of the most interesting areas of Glasgow as we find people and places...

IN YOUR NEIGHBOURHOOD

GLASGOWIST HAS WRITten a lot about Finnieston in the last five years. You'll find mentions of the area throughout this book. A collection of businesses around a focused stretch of Argyle Street has seen the name become a byword of a new wave of Glasgow confidence and personality.

There's a curious thing that happens when we mention Finnieston. Some people can get very animated when it comes to the boundaries of the area, which is wedged in tight amidst a cluster of long standing neighbourhoods. They don't like the name used like a slogan.

We actually submitted a formal

FINNIESTON

question to the council once asking them to define the area but they demurred, referring to the fact burgh wards no longer exist. We then turned to a higher power, Norry Wilson from the Lost Glasgow Facebook group: "Aye, all these old area distinctions are fairly fluid. And remember, Partick didn't even become part of Glasgow until 1912. The village of Finnieston was established in 1768 on the lands of Stobcross by Matthew Orr, the

Argyle Street is the main artery of one of Glasgow's coolest neighbourhoods.

Ox & Finch for steak and a glass of wine.

COLIN TEMPLETON

owner of Stobcross House. Orr named the new village Finnieston in honour of the Reverend John Finnie, who had been his tutor."

So where to start with this modern version of the village? The Pub. Strip Joint to be precise, across from the statue of Charles Rennie Mackintosh and close to the alluring panini of Accento Cafe.

The name is a wry nod to the fact Argyle Street started to be referred to as the Finnieston Strip some time after the construction of The Hydro. The sun streams through the windows on a sunny day and you have a steady supply of craft beer, cocktails, pizza and a vinyl collection. It's our pre-gig meeting point.

You can sit outside Tajura Cafe, grab a coffee and read a book - just make sure it's a suitably hefty tome, you will be judged. The Brass Monkey is another great local and had a previous life as the Two Ways, the pub in Rab C Nesbitt.

Gallus Alice is a bright and

breezy independent clothes shop as we move further along the street. Across from Blow, Glasgow's most stylish hairdressers, there's a wee window where you can get a cup of homemade soup from Soula to takeaway.

The Grove Fish & Chips will do you a single supper - or you could get a roll and deep-fried square sausage from The Kent. Let's pause beside The Finnieston bar and restaurant. The building is part of local history - it was a drovers inn, one that Rob Roy MacGregor is said to have frequented. These days, it's a seafood and cocktail destination with a gin garden out the back. Across the road, The Crescent will mix you up a cocktail.

Porter & Rye for a relaxed steak dinner. Rebel Rebel for a haircut. Roots & Fruits for groceries. The Ben Nevis, Six by Nico, The Gannet, Kelvingrove Cafe, Rioja. There's a lot going on.

If you stretch Finnieston out a wee bit, The Park Bar and The Islay

THE HIDDEN LANE

THROUGH A TUNNEL OFF ARGYLE Street, swerving away from the Finnieston crowds, you will find an alternative shopping experience at The Hidden Lane. There are more than 100 studios hosting local designers, musicians, jewellers, guitar makers and writers. Situated in a neighbouring warehouse, The Hive is a honeypot of hairdressers, massage therapists and yoga instructors.

In recent years, this collective has grown in popularity with locals and registered on the radar of visitors. Cobbled courtyards and stained-glass windows are overlooked by tenements, juxtaposing the urban bursts of colour, lightbulbs and rainbow bunting. This patchwork of once semi-derelict garages and stables was revived by Joe Mulholland and his late wife, Claire.

The Lane continues to bloom. Plans have recently been approved to transform an empty workshop into a restaurant. The Hidden Lane Brewery is now in place. The plan is to continue to increase footfall to this neighbourhood pedestrianised quarter.

"Our tenants are often creative, always individual and they have an independent spirit and desire to succeed on their own terms that makes life in The Lane always interesting.

"The Lane reflects the ethos of Glasgow most, perhaps, in its friendliness, quirkiness and eagerness to please" says Carole Dunlop, Hidden Lane & Hive Co-ordinator.

You could easily pass an afternoon blethering with artisans and retailers, nibbling on fruit scones at The Hidden Lane Cafe, wandering through the backstreets, admiring original design pieces, perusing shabby-chic trinkets or taking classes in pottery, floristry and embroidery. More than just visual creation, The Lane also hosts a radio station, live music performances, and production studios responsible for the outputs of acts including Snow Patrol and Franz Ferdinand.

Dunlop adds: "Visitors can feel good about supporting home-grown innovation and entrepreneurship. The pandemic has tipped the scales away from globalisation and chain businesses which can only be a good thing for places like The Lane.

"When you shop local a real person really does do a 'happy dance' - you are making a difference to the life of that business owner or creative and to the local economy and vibrancy of Finnieston."

📍 *1103 Argyle Street, G3 8ND*
🌐 *thehiddenlaneglasgow.com*

Words: Amy Lyall

Rebel Rebel is your local barber

Inn are two of the great traditional bars in the city and great favourites of local highlanders.

A special mention for the Finnieston Tree. It's around 160 years old, and over four storeys tall. We'll let Stuart Murdoch of Belle and Sebastian describe it: "This is one of the key Glasgow trees. They used to call it 'The Only Tree in Argyle Street'. It's a north facing ash rammed up against the tenements. It must have good genes to have made it! It's hip now, because it's in Finnieston, but I say it was always cool."

Five From the Lane

SPIN POTTERY
An independent ceramic studio offering crafty parties, pottery classes and the chance to make clay prints. The team also take commissions and host a shop featuring work by local artists.
⬮ *spinpotteryglasgow*

HOUSE OF BLACK
Revamping damaged clothing, recycling unwanted apparel and repurposing fabric cuttings (often donated by fellow Hidden Lane residents), this Glasgow-based fashion brand strives to create stylish zero-waste garments.
🌐 *houseofblk.co.uk*

BOBBIN & FLECK
It all started with a mid-century furniture love affair. Pop into this craft workshop offering upholstery, cane work, soft furnishing, fabrics, wood finishing and repairs.
🌐 *bobbinandfleck.com*

FINNIESTON YOGA SHALA
Find your inner Zen in this community-centric studio. Fully qualified instructors lead Ashtanga, Yin and Vinyasa yoga classes for all levels, starting from absolute beginner.
⬮ *finniestonyogashala*

BRIAR ROSE DESIGN
Wedding bouquets, funeral flowers and corporate creations, this sustainable florist takes inspiration from changing seasons and historical folklore to craft her largely Scottish-grown designs. Floral workshops are also offered.
🌐 *briarroseflowers.co.uk*

VICTORIA ROAD IS ONE OF the city's great thoroughfares, running right down the middle of the Southside and connecting its many neighbourhoods. It's a multicultural area which has, over the years, been a hub of activity for different migrant communities, and it always feels like it's moving forward.

Even if you know Glasgow's neighbourhoods well, if you've been over there recently, you will surely have been struck by the pace of change. Starting at the bottom of the road – at the edge of Queen's Park, let's take a walk around some of the interesting local places you might want to discover.

VICTORIA ROAD

First, a choice. What side of the street? To the left, the Queen's Park Cafe; and on the right: the Queen's Cafe. Confused? You will be. They're not cafes. The former is a classic Glasgow boozer and the latter is technically now Ginesi's ice cream – they kept the old sign for posterity. Assuming it's not yet beer o'clock, go right and get some proper Italian gelato with flavours like hazelnut, gianduja and vegan salted caramel.

Cross the road and pop into Some Great Reward – a petite but comprehensive little indie vinyl store – and then Sacred Tum, one of the surprisingly few places in this city you can find a good taco. ST's are simple and vibrant, so apple cabbage slaw cuts through crispy pork, while pickle aioli adds sharp acidity to flaky cod.

Get buzzed at Short Long Black

Back on the other side of the road, drift onto Dixon Avenue and into The Bell Jar. It's a pub from the same folk who own Partick's Sparklehorse, and a gratefully received addition to the neighborhood since it opened in 2018. Gastropub small plates are on the menu. Think seabass with cherry tomato; or duck filo parcels. It's just one of those places that's comfortably cool, and great to go for a pint. So do that. Further down the same road is Flower, a vegan bakery with a rugged aesthetic and a fantastic understanding of how to get the most out of olive oils and Middle Eastern flavours in their breads, cakes and pies. Well worth the brief detour.

Back on Vicky Road and your coffee options explode: first up, Short Long Black – a slender cafe with strong caffeine credentials. Transylvania is a Romanian spot selling cakes like Carpathian custard and cherry, as well as a hefty

If it's later in the day, and you're lucky enough to get in, Errol's Hot Pizza – pairing New York-style crispy bases with some modern Mediterranean influences in a quirky little space – epitomises the DIY demeanour of the area.

Several fruit and veg stalls spill out onto the street, and butchers (both halal and otherwise) are also easily found. Then there's Locavore, an organic and rigorously-sourced grocery store with a thriving veg box subscription scheme and an in-store cafe. Like Milk, they're a social enterprise and all profits go back into working towards a better local food system.

Walk up Calder Street and you'll see Govanhill Baths, a Edwardian bath house – Glasgow's last – rescued from demolition that's now a community trust aiming to ultimately restore the baths to a modern version of their former glory, whilst energising the area through a myriad range of initiatives promoting health, inclusivity and cultural diversity. Just up from that, you can sample proper Pakistani comfort food at Yadgar - their combination of massive flavours and understated home cooking is pretty fantastic.

By now you're thoroughly in Govanhill – but if you were to double back and cross Victoria Road you'd be in Strathbungo and Pollokshields territory, where Kurdish Street Food, Little Hanoi and The Rum Shack give you spicy shawarma, punchy Vietnamese flavours and zingy Caribbean dishes like chicken brown down, respectively. If the purist in you wanted to end on Victoria Road itself, there are a couple of outposts at the very end including Bar Vini, a snazzy wee Italian spot doing antipasti and pasta with class and panache . And that's it. The Vicky Road. Done. Until the next new place opens up, which has probably already happened...

Words: David Kirkwood

range of Eastern European meats and confectionery. A few doors up is Milk, a social enterprise that looks to empower and support migrant and refugee women living in Glasgow – a lovely place for a coffee that exists for all sorts of the right reasons. The mural inside (from Glaswegian artist Catherine Weir) is a thing of joy, and initiatives like their takeaway supper club (week 1: Lebanon, week 2: Kerala, and so on), are constantly evolving celebrations of the cuisines and cultures of the women that they work with.

A further wander and you're starting to reach the charity shops, and if thrift stores are your thing, give yourself a good hour to delve in. You might want to briefly hang a left on Allison Street and see Alex Coyle's mural of Scott Hutchison, the dearly missed singer of Frightened Rabbit. It was painted to raise awareness of Tiny Changes, the charity set up in his name.

We're at the business end of the stretch now – especially for food. There's Patricia's, (from the Short Long Black team) for loaded breakfast brioche or eggs Benedict served on buttery sourdough.

Errol's Hot Pizza for a slice of the neighbourhood.

My Glasgow

GEORGE BOWIE
Clyde 1 presenter, GBX

I LOVE THE PARTY ATMOSPHERE of Glasgow. You've got to be yourself. You can't get away with faking it in Glasgow which is always good. We have the best atmosphere for clubs and for gigs. I meet DJs all the time and they say it's the best. The difference between here and elsewhere is night and day. We played down south and thought it was not a good gig and promoters have said you've absolutely smashed it.

When I was a kid my mum would take me into town to Fraser's or the big stores to see Santa and I remember going on the underground for the first time was an amazing experience. I always remember that as a wee guy.

I live in the West End, so I love all the eateries on Byres Road and the ones on Queen Margaret Drive. I go out all the time for food because I don't get much of a chance to see my kids at the weekend cause I'm always working then.

When people go out at the week-

end I'm doing radio shows and clubs so I go to places like Elois cafe on Queen Margaret Drive, the Albanian place. I like that. We go to William Cafe every Sunday and right now I'm off to Little Italy on Byres Road which is my daughter's favourite restaurant.

In terms of shopping in the city, we do have our own style in Glasgow but, I'll be honest, I'm rubbish at picking clothes. Ellen picks all my clothes for me because I look ridiculous when I choose something. She's great at that. We have always been clothes-conscious here.

It's funny. When I first moved to the City of Glasgow from Kilmalcolm, the wee village, in the late eighties, I thought I'll need to get my act together with clothes. It was a wake up call with my fashion. I thought "what's happening here?"

For relaxing I go to the Botanics all the time. I'm always there because it's five minutes from my house and I've got a dog. You get to meet a lot of people. I've made a lot of friends here in the area I live and we all go out at roughly the same time.

I would go to a few of the open air bars like Sanctuary, that's a good one. Some of the ones in Ashton Lane I enjoy. I don't drink very often so I go for coffee.

I genuinely don't

William Cafe (left) George Bowie on the decks.

think there is anywhere else like Glasgow. I think its a unique city and I've always called it the biggest village in Europe because it is like that where everybody knows everybody.

It's bizarre how everybody knows one another and knows what everybody is up to and all that kind of stuff.

We are very loyal to our own and we get that with the radio station, how many people just listen in because we are a radio station based in Glasgow.

The architecture is beautiful too, amazing. It's a great place and we should be happy and proud of it. I couldn't live anywhere else in the world. We moan about the weather and I hate the rain but you put up with it because everywhere else is so great.

Pancakes, poached eggs and pots of tea.
Join the breakfast club and start your day at
one of these quirky neighbourhood spots.

GLASGOW'S TOP 5
BRUNCHES

1 Cafe Strange Brew

Owner and chef Laurie MacMillan has redefined what it means to be a Glasgow neighbourhood cafe over the last five years while creating a Shawlands landmark in Cafe Strange Brew. Its reputation spans far beyond the Southside. Pancakes

have been their signature dish but the waffle-maker has been put to good use with innovative specials like sweet potato waffle with hoisin duck and fried egg. Salt beef Benedict with sauerkraut, dill pickle and mustard hollandaise also defies expectations. More recently there's been breakfast rolls to takeaway and loaded flatbreads and fruity vegan dishes. They'll always have something for your weekend.

📍 1082 Pollokshaws Road, G41 3XA
f cafestrangebrew

2 Singl-end

On a Saturday, we order the meaty baked eggs, a casserole of homemade pork and fennel sausage, cannellini beans, tomato and chilli built around the aforementioned eggs. It's morning comfort food as an art form, to be excavated from a warm skillet. The Cure Yer Heid smoothie of strawberries, raspberries, blackberries, banana and ginger mixed with orange juice is good for what ails you. As is a bottle of crisp, dry Rosato rosé wine. When you've finished all that, linger a bit longer in this oasis of calm and conversation before you rejoin the fray. Go to the cake table and pick out a slice of millionaire's shortbread. Order another pot of tea. Finish telling that story. The rest of the weekend can wait.

📍 263 Renfrew Street, G3 6TT
🌐 thesingl-end.co.uk

3 Partick Duck Club

A bit about the name: There was a tavern that stood on Old Dumbarton Road, a favourite of a group of Glasgow merchants and professors. In 1810 they formed the Duck Club of Partick and would dine each Saturday on local roast duck from the River Kelvin, served with sage and onion with green peas, and washed down with pints of ale. Not a bad way to spend the weekend. These days, stellar brunch options include shakshuka baked eggs on sourdough, flaky smoked salmon with scrambled eggs or the 24 hour beef shin and duck egg Benedict. Always order a side of duck fat fries.

📍 27 Hyndland Street, G11 5QF
🌐 partickduckclub.co.uk

4 Epicures by Cail Bruich

A team up between the Oli Norman owned Epicures and fine dining restaurant Cail Bruich has brought the brunch buzz back to Hyndland. A bright and airy space for a leisurely bite to eat and a few drinks with pals. Start off with a morning roll or order a slew of Cumbrae oysters, depending on what kind of day you are having. We also like their smoked salmon on rye and ale bread, cream cheese and a sprinkling of caviar. Freshly baked breads, cakes and pastries to takeaway. Don't leave without a cronut.

📍 159 Hyndland Road, G12 9JA
🌐 epicures.co.uk

5 Gnom

Known for their playful, experimental and global approach to food, Gnom have established themselves as Strathbungo's brunch destination. A relaxed bistro, they also serve homemade cakes, locally sourced teas and their own Gnom coffee blend. Look for their homemade rowie buns: "Scottish croissant type things, stuffed with N'duja sausage and pesto or charred spring onion, pesto and Parmesan". Expect bao buns and Turkish eggs on the weekend menu.

📍 758 Pollokshaws Road, G41 2AE
f gnomfood

I'M SITTING OUTSIDE THE SPAR-
kle Horse, holding a glass of
rum as the sun starts to dip
behind the tenements. It's a
crisp drink infused with full-on flavours, real ingredients and spices.
It was made in Partick.

"When we were develop-
ing the recipe, we took a spiced
rum and stripped it right back
down and built it back up again.
There's heaps of fresh ginger in
there, fresh lime peel, orange
peel, nutmeg, cardamom, vanilla,
cloves, a few other spices as well"
Zander Macgregor tells me from
across the table. He set up Wester
Spirit Co with his friend Allan
Nairn and a sense of adventure.

Their story shows how parts of
the city can foster and encourage
new ideas and businesses. There's
a buzz to Partick right now: Wee
quirky shops, neighbourhood restaurants, art studios, workshops.
Wester took inspiration from that

Riverside Museum and the Glenlee

manent about the sight of Partick
around Dumbarton Road with
Glasgow University looming in the
distance. You'll spot a comforting
number of red T's outside pubs
that have stood for generations.

Partick has been in existence
since David I granted lands around
1136. A village until the mid-1700s,
the Kings of Strathclyde had a base
here. The traditional red stone tenements sprawl from the former
Western Infirmary along Dumbar-

Patrick. There's also a charming
library, which was built in 1925.

If you're travelling by Subway
to Patrick, look out for Ranald
MacColl's G.I. Bride statue – a
character created by Bud Neill, the
famous Glasgow cartoonist, as
part of the Lobey Dosser cowboy
comic strip that ran in the Evening
Times in the 1950s.

After the hustle and bustle of
Dumbarton Road, head up the hill
and along Hyndland Road. Visit
Cafezique for fantastic French
toast or pick up a coffee from
KAF. Patrick Duck Club has been
making a name for itself since
opening in 2017. Go for a great gin
and tonic and the best chips in the
West End. Pick up fresh fruit and
veg from the Polish supermarket
or Ashby's.

Fresh flowers and plants can be
seen in eye-catching displays from
Lavender Blue, and at the top of
the hill, looming large over the
neighbourhood is Cottiers Theatre, Bar and Restaurant – based in
the converted Dowanhill Church
and named after architect, Daniel
Cottier.

At the lower end of Partick is
the Riverside Museum – Glasgow's
Transport Museum, which was
designed by architect Zaha Hadid
and opened in 2011, having been
previously located in the Kelvin
Hall building. Following on the
transport theme, next to the Riverside Museum is The Tall Ship
Glenlee, a Clyde-built sailing ship
berthed at Pointhouse Quay.

After a day exploring, find the
perfect slice of pizza at Basta on
Dumbarton Road. Chef owner
Jane Chalmers says: "We've fairly
traditional pizzas on the menu.
The more popular ones
are the specials that we
work on in the kitchen.
Our first was Irn Bru
ham and pineapple,
finished with a blow-
torch. Our version of a
Partick Hawaiian."

PARTICK

emerging scene and grew alongside it. You can arrange to visit
them at their distillery on Meadow
Road.

"There's a really vibrant cultural
scene in Glasgow. We want to tap
into that and work with all the
local businesses around Meadow
Road to make that area a hub
of independent producers. The
city has a fantastic bar scene too.
Hopefully people want to try new
things, and Glasgow rum can make
a name for itself as a quality spirit"
Zander says.

On the north bank of the River
Clyde, opposite Govan, change has
come to this pocket of the West
End, but there's something per-

ton Road and past Byres Road to
just beyond Crow Road. The area
is a hotpotch of different shops,
eateries and businesses. Browse
flooring, get a shirt tailored, then
pop into a hardware store before
getting your nails or hair done.

The Lismore pub at Partick
Cross is a favourite with the
folk and trad scene. Further
down the road, the Deoch
An Dorus is a classic pub for
a hawf and hawf. The Three
Judges pub sells a fine selection of cask ales.

One of the main areas of
Glasgow with strong links
to the Highlands, the Gaelic
Books Council is located in

The GI Bride waits eternally at Partick subway station

Dumbarton Road towards Glasgow University

IT CAN BE HARD TO KNOW where to start with Maryhill, or the 'Venice of the North', as it's affectionately known in this part of the city. The area might not be on everyone's list of Glasgow hotspots, but it has depth and character like few other places, and like its Italian counterpart it has canals – or one, at least.

For a historic burgh that has weathered industrial decline, there is plenty that is preserved and repackaged for the present. And counter-intuitively, it is one of the best places within the city to escape the city.

Both the River Kelvin and the picturesque Forth and Clyde Canal run through its heart. Otters and deer are frequent visitors to its fringes, just minutes from its busy streets and roads.

In sport, the area is home to Glasgow's third or first football team, depending how you look at it. Firhill, the home of Partick Thistle, sits in a kink in the river, a theatre of emotions surrounded by wildlife and city schemes.

For the rootsier sports fan, Maryhill FC is the amateur team to follow.

When in Maryhill, plot a route along its eponymous high street, its canal paths and riverside.

Local landmarks abound. D'Jaconelli's Cafe has been used as a film and television location for productions including *Trainspotting* starring local boy Robert Carlyle and cult TV series *Tutti Frutti*, featuring Robbie Coltrane.

Up the way, the tower blocks of Collina Street were the fictional home of Scotland's greatest pensioner pals, Jack and Victor from *Still Game*.

Maryhill Burgh Halls is a heritage and exhibition space opened in 2012 after the building was saved from demolition and given a new purpose.

Similarly, across the road, The Engine Works, an imposing refur-

MARYHILL

bished industrial space is now a wonderful event venue waiting for the good times to return.

Charles Rennie Mackintosh's only church, Queen's Cross, is a city jewel. It's on Garscube Road.

Every year in early spring, the canal welcomes endurance swimmers to the Neptune Steps event as they power along a stretch of water between the locks.

Rubber-clad souls push stamina to the limit on a gruelling course of freezing water, rope ladders and sheer-sided walls.

A more sedate pastime is taking in the waters of the River Kelvin as they head west towards the sur-

City lights at Maryhill Burgh Halls

prisingly spectacular Garscube Estate and Dawsholm local nature reserve.

In recent years, the Maryhill Integration Network has been helping the many people arriving in Scotland as refugees and asylum seekers from all parts of the world.

Nicola McHendry, heritage development and community engagement manager at the Burgh Halls, says: "Maryhill is really vibrant and diverse.

"We have a huge variety of different people in the area, from students, communities in places like the Wyndford flats, young and old people, and lots of people from

ANDREW LEE

B Y THE TIME LATE-VICTORIAN architects and developers got around to laying out Hyndland, Glasgow had perfected the art of tenement building.

The district's fine built heritage is a distinguishing feature that sets it apart from other areas of the city.

In little over a dozen years, between 1898 and 1910, its distinctive central grid of streets and lanes were formed out of Dumfriesshire red sandstone in the fields around Hind Land farm.

The railway spur that today is Old Station Park was the conduit by which materials

nurture the local sense of belonging.

"I have been here for more than 30 years, and I love Hyndland with a passion. It is like a village and when you have been here for as long as I have you become part of that."

Ken Main who co-owns a hair salon on Hydland Road with wife Ellen Conlin agrees the area has a special quality. His family had a delicatessen in Clarence Drive many years ago, before delis were even fashionable.

"I was brought up on Clarence Drive and lived in Dudley Drive initially. I went to Hyndland Primary School and then to Hillhead High, so I know the area.

"Hyndland is an eclectic mix of houses

HYNDLAND

came in to rapidly expand the housing stock.

Then, the area was popular with merchants and the professions that were swelling in number under the city's burgeoning wealth. Hyndland continues to be a popular location for academics at the city's universities, lawyers and the creative fraternity. It is not uncommon to spy a familiar face from the worlds of TV, comedy or sport browsing its shopfronts. The BBC Club had a former home on Hyndland Road and the connection endures.

The parade of boutique shops, independent cafes, bistros and bars make it an attractive part of town for a wander.

Hyndland shouldn't be dismissed as an exclusively middle-class enclave in a post-industrial city. The area is more nuanced than that. It's secondary school, for instance, is local authority run and covers one of the most diverse catchments in the city. Nearly a third of its students are from neighbouring areas such as Thornwood and Whiteinch which are in the lowest income parts of Scotland.

Hyndland also displays close community values. A summer gala brings people together during August in two of the local parks. Business owners like Marco Stevenson at Pizza Magic on Hyndland Road

1051 GWR is a popular neighbourhood bar and restaurant

different parts of the world.

"It's a great community, and for such a small area there's an awful lot going on and there's a lot of green space. I think it surprises a lot of people."

New restaurants and businesses when they do open are welcomed, such as The Botany on Maryhill Road.

Aria Gaughan, a manager at the bar, says: "The canal walks and the community are what makes Maryhill special and people are very keen to support local businesses.

"Customers are very varied from 'Maryhillians' that have been here for years to young families and students. It's a diverse area to live and work in."

With its football, waterways, local history, buildings and strong personality, Maryhill is a snapshot of Glasgow in miniature.

Words: Ian Marland

and shops and the attraction I've always thought is that everything is within walking distance."

And indeed, the best way to enjoy the neighbourhood is on foot. One route from the bar and restaurant 1051 GWR, takes you along Great Western Road towards the elegant Hotel Du Vin on Devonshire Gardens.

The walk takes in local sports clubs, Hillhead and Western, which are more inclusive than their postcode may suggest. The Western tennis club, for instance, works heavily with schools and families in Maryhill to bring the sport to people who would not normally get involved.

Hyndland is full of beautiful buildings and spaces, best seen on foot and with an open mind.

Words: Ian Marland

I WOKE UP THIS MORNING IN THE eighth coolest neighbourhood in the world, according to Time Out's annual survey. It's an unexpected level of recognition for this enclave in the East End, centred around Duke Street and Alexandria Parade with the Drives in between.

I remember talking to long term Dennistoun resident and broadcaster Stuart Cosgrove about the changes locally and influx of new residents: "There's an awful lot of people who have moved into Dennistoun because it's a great place to come for a starter house, or a flat if you can't afford the West End and Finnieston. So there's a young bohemian element to it. And that's all fine. I can live with that. I'm not exactly against someone having a pointed beard and a Harris tweed suit. It's not going to change my life" he said.

Having been sequestered in Dennistoun since March, I know that businesses facing their own hardship continued to work

DENNISTOUN

together to support those in need among their neighbours. Food businesses operated a network to share resources and to deliver care packages. Local church groups maintained food banks and contact with those that were shielding. It's important to judge an area on its character, not just

the availability of sourdough bread, good coffee and craft beers.

Mesa, my local brunch place (order the Italian sausage, cannellini, potato hash with herbs, topped with a fried egg) is one of the businesses enlivening the neighbourhood.

I asked co-owner Laurie Mac-

Millan, who also has Sweet Jane Bakehouse here, what she makes of it all: She said: "There's never a dull day in Dennistoun. It's diverse. It's multicultural and, at times, it's completely off its rocker.

"You will find the real Glasgow here, the nitty gritty, the warm and the wonderful. Strong sense

COLIN MEARNS

Coia's Cafe is at the heart of the neighbourhood

Paul Trainer at Roslea Drive. The Best of Glasgow was written on this street.

one of the local brunch bunch. Tibo is a long-standing neighbourhood cafe where you can pop in for a coffee, cure a hangover with their Stornoway Stack breakfast or assemble a selection of small plates for a long lunch. Bookies, booze shops and barbers remain prevalent the further you go down Duke Street, but you will also find pretty epic burgers at Dennistoun BBQ. Currently open for takeaway.

East Coffee Company have their roastery and cafe here, providing excellent bagels and coffee. There's Zero Waste Market for environmentally friendly groceries. You'll also spot curious wee shops like The Repairman on Hillfoot Street where you can get your telly fixed if you can make your way inside around all the assembled bric-a-brac. Elsewhere, Scran is a popular cafe on Alexandra Parade. Celino's and Coia's compete to be the favourite neighbourhood Italian. Walk off your pasta dinner by going to Alexandra Park, just watch out for stray golf balls from the municipal course.

Bilson Eleven is a small, family run fine dining restaurant in the front room of a townhouse on Annfield Place. It has been included in the Michelin Guide, with the food described as "interesting and original with a playful edge". You'll find confident cooking, exceptional local produce and a bit of East End personality.

Words: Paul Trainer

of community and some loveable rogues to boot. Pull up a pew and watch life go by on Duke Street."

Dennistoun has a curious mix of grand individual houses that sit close to the Tennent's Brewery on the border towards town and long stretches of handsome tenements.

Looking around the neighbourhood, there's a collection of food and drink places that are worth a visit. Redmond's is one of the founding members of Dennistoun's cool new wave. You'll find a warm welcome, a fine selection of craft beer, ramen, gyoza and impressive bao buns. Rawnchy

Mesa for breakfast

sits just outside the main stretch of Duke Street. When Poppy Murricane moved to Dennistoun, she created one of the city's best raw food and vegan cafes here. Now serving a new savoury menu and

THE BARRAS IS A PLACE that exists in Glasgow's imagination as much as it is an actual market in the East End of the city, sitting between The Gallowgate and London Road. It occupies a particular part of the Glasgow psyche, invoking colourful images of traders and shoppers that conform to an idea of what Glaswegians are all about and have shades of nostalgia for a vanishing city.

In reality, The Barras and Calton have sat on the periphery of the city centre behind invisible barriers for decades. The area is now awakening from slumber and has new opportunities.

At The Barras, the familiar market stalls hawking bric-a-brac and secondhand items have been joined by more street food operators, musicians, design, fashion and artist collectives. New businesses are opening. People are moving into the area. Barriers are

old meets new. The list of pub landlords stretches back to 1838. When the building was being restored last year, workers uncovered layers of local history. There's part of an original Tongs Ya Bas menchy on the wall behind the bar, remnants of a tenemental past. We're told there's at least a couple of folk in each week claiming to have been the ones that wrote it. During lockdown, the bar was converted into a community kitchen, working with other local groups to feed disadvantaged families across the city.

If you are having a wander around, look out for the Barras Pirate mural by Rogue One at

The backyard at BAaD.

CALTON

being broken down. The streetscape has been transformed by smart paving stones and more public areas.

The Gallowgate is far from the place that Matt McGinn once sang about, and yet this feels more like a revival than displacement. The community still faces deprivation and social problems, but the Calton Barras Action Plan – a major intervention in funding by Glasgow City Council and the Scottish Government, started in 2013 – aims to change that.

When Saint Luke's opened as a music venue, it was a clarion call to others who have made this their part of the city. 226 Gallowgate, beside the Barrowland Ballroom, is a community bar where

the back of The Old Burnt Barns pub. Visit Polski supermarket on Gallowgate for Polish sweets and groceries or Polish Taste on London Road for meats, cheeses and pierogi. Bill's Tool Store is one of the most famous businesses in the area and is the place to go for

Mussels on the menu at Calton Taproom

all your DIY equipment.

Arti San Toi on Moncur Street sells one-of-a-kind artworks and is a meeting spot for artists with character. Go to The Rumbling Tum on the corner of Gallowgate and Bain Street for a roll and sausage with a cup of tea.

Across the road, Barras Art and Design has become one of the city's most popular venues, hosting gigs by international artists, food markets, techno parties, football on the big screen, creative conferences and now it is the home to the Calton Taproom. The venue, with outdoor space for 200 people, brings together local craft brews and a fantastic barbecue food and small plate menu featuring slow-cooked, rotisserie and grilled dishes. There is also a recently installed Mezcal bar upstairs that's worth investigating. In the Taproom itself, choose from 20 different local select crafts on rotation, featuring brewers from the west of Scotland and further afield. Closer to Glasgow Green, Whistler on the Green gastropub is due to open before the end of the year on Greendyke Street.

Through the Lens

Hudson Martins Ribeiro was born in Brazil, raised in Sweden and is now part of things here in Glasgow. Hudson's goal is to "show a more cinematic Scotland". He works as the Head of FX at prestigious animation company Axis Studios, based on Elliot Street, while indulging his enthusiasm for photography. This is his photograph of West End towers, looking over from Garnethill.

"I moved here five years ago, I wanted the job with the studios so I could work on Halo, my favourite game. I soon made a connection with Glasgow. I like how diverse and beautiful the West End is, you see old buildings, ones you know people will never build like that again, then you have the modern aspects. It's that mix. The buildings are still full of life and I think that's important.

"I love telling stories through photographs. I saw all these beautiful surroundings and I wanted to show it to everyone, the way I see it."

See more pictures of Glasgow:
⬡ *hudsonmartinsribeiro* ⬤ *hudsonmartins.com*

The Winter Gardens

SPRINGBURN PARK OCCUpies the highest point in the City of Glasgow and opened in 1892. The Reid family funded construction of the spectacular Winter Gardens and people would travel from all over to this oasis of greenery that at one point had model yacht ponds, tennis courts, a cricket oval, hockey pitch and bowling rinks. At the start of the 20th Century Springburn was a powerhouse of industrial expansion, with locomotive works building powerful tank engines to be exported across the world.

Much of old Springburn is gone. 85 per cent of its buildings were demolished and 40 per cent of its population moved as an expressway was cut through the area in the 1970s and 80s. A further reminder of the past, the Public Halls, was demolished in 2012. Springburn Park continues to be a focus for the local community and in recent years there has been attempts to revive its fortunes.

The Springburn Winter Gardens Trust is determined to restore the historic structure which has lain derelict since 1983. Designs have been sketched that could see the striking framework transformed into a performance space with meeting rooms and a café bar.

Paul Sweeney was a founding member of the Trust: "I've always had a fascination with the history of the area since I got this book called Old Springburn. I'd sit with my granddad going through it and listening to stories. The thing that got me as a kid was, "I don't recognise any of this. None of it's there anymore."

"After the Public Halls went, I started talking to people about making sure the same doesn't happen to the Winter Gardens. They were related to each other. The Reid Family were the main locomotive industrialists in Springburn. They lived in a man-

SPRINGBURN PARK

Creating a piano auditorium as a new community resource.

sion called Belmont House at the end of Springburn Park. Basically, it was their front garden. They sponsored the creation of the park donated all sorts of public buildings around Springburn when it became part of Glasgow in the 1890s."

"We've raised money and we were able to do structural repairs in 2017 to ensure the frame of the roof was secured. There's also a Friends of Springburn Park group that works on maintaining the park grounds in general. They've most recently created a new 40 seat auditorium made from recycled pianos in an old Romney shed in the park, in collaboration with Glasgow Piano City to create a small venue for the north of the city."

The Winter Gardens was the largest single-span glass house in Scotland. The building's design is based on a train shed, a nod towards the local railway. "Originally, there were a lot of glasshouses on either side of it. They were used to grow all the bedding plants for every park in Glasgow" Paul says.

In 2016, Joan Reid, the granddaughter of Sir Hugh Reid, chairman of the North British Locomotive Company, handed over a treasure trove of family artefacts to the city that had been sealed in a safety deposit box in a local lawyer's office since the 1930s. They included silver and gold caskets gifted by Glasgow Corporation to Sir Hugh containing his 1917 Freedom of the City scroll. The Trust hope that one day these items might be displayed within a renovated Winter Gardens, restoring Spingburn's connection to its history.

My Glasgow

ANDY CAMERON
Broadcaster & entertainer

THE WORD "GALLUS" IS SYNonymous with Glasgow. I've never heard of it used in any other city. There is a swagger here. Throw anything at us. We'll either bat it away or overcome it. There is a community spirit in Glasgow from either side of any divide that is there. There is a common thought whether you are blue or green, Muslim or Christian, you are living in the same city and that fact makes you stick together. That's special about Glasgow.

I guess most cities in the world now have trains or tram cars in the streets. In 1962 they took away the tramcars and that took a bit of Glasgow away. I always remember being on the tram and people would talk to one another as if they all were from one house.

I lived in Rutherglen growing up and I remember going to the football at Hampden Park and you'd say "Mister, can you lift us over" at the barrier. That's where you'd learn to swear. You could walk down to Shawfield Stadium where Clyde played, and they also had the dog tracks. I still think about those things although a lot is no longer there. Try to explain that to your grandchildren, that this bit or that bit used to be full of tenements.

I remember as a wee boy we had a teacher, Miss Peters at Fairy Street School. We went to see a boat being launched – the SS Windsor – at Connell's yard. We went to Victoria Park for a picnic. Six years after the war finished. Every time I pass it I think about it.

They had a green in Rutherglen in Waverley Street, and we played football there as kids. The Scottish Championship was held there around 1948 and we were two closes down from it. There must have been twenty young boys up the top of the washhouse looking down on it. It's a fantas-

tic memory. I can still smell the tobacco and the beer from when we collected the empties after it.

My gran used to run a menodge savings club for Margaret Forrester Drapers on London Road. It was a huge store, and everyone gave her a pound and every week one of the twenty had twenty pounds to spend. It was a great thing.

I've got a lot of pals who used to have pubs but are now retired so that choice has gone. I'm not much of a drinker anyway. Nowadays, if I'm heading out, I'll go to Finnieston because there is a really good restaurant every two yards. Crabshakk and others have just come up over the last ten years. Mother India is fantastic and I remember Gibson Street when Indian food first came to Glasgow in the late fifties and early and you'd get a curry at the Shish Mahal. They say Birmingham is meant to be the curry capital, but Glasgow gives it a run for its money.

Lewis's, where Debenhams now is, used to have a record store in the basement and you'd go down and buy Fats Domino records. At sixteen years of age, way ahead of my time, I bought Frank Sinatra's *Songs for Swinging Lovers* and I

Finnieston's Crabshakk is a firm favourite

remember going into a booth and listening to it on earphones.

People still go to Slater's to get clothes. It used to be Burtons or Jackson the tailors and you'd get measured. You could pay it up but you'd get a brand new suit after six weeks. There was an expression, "Get him, he looks like he just stepped out of Jackson's windae".

I'm eighty now. Every city has its own identity. For Glaswegians it is really strong. I look back and think, "Wow, my grandchildren will never experience it the way I did". The shoogly tramcars at Dalmuir West or Springburn to Burnside. They had a particular feel and smell. Last year I took my grandchildren from Spain to the transport museum. They couldn't believe the Coronation tram with a point at the end. If they brought them back, maybe they wouldn't be as shoogly now.

NICK PONTY

57

Great Western Road, one of
Glasgow's best streets

HUDSON MARTINS RIBEIRO

GREAT WESTERN ROAD

JOE LAZZERINI AND HIS partner Amalia Colaluca opened the doors to The Loveable Rogue on Great Western Road late in the summer. Both have a background in hospitality, but this is their first venture together. When they embarked on the project, they had no idea how events would play out this year.

Amalia says: "We decided to work together when the opportunity came up to take over The Hebridean. We wanted to change things over to The Loveable Rogue before the summer and were moving towards that, but with covid restrictions it wasn't possible. This is us now doing what we wanted to do. Joe and I are partners both personally and now professionally. I work front of house and Joe runs the kitchen. To have our own pub restaurant, this is our dream".

Who is the most loveable and who is the most roguish? "Amalia is loveable and I'm a bit of a rogue I suppose" Joe laughs. "Joe has a heart of gold but the story behind the name is probably more about him" Amalia says.

The menu focuses on what you would expect from a good Glasgow pub. Comfort food like ox cheek pie or black pudding with apple or rabbit rarebit. There is lobster mac n' cheese and monkfish scampi. The Sunday roast lunch is popular.

We talk around what they hope

to do with the place and they've both got a real enthusiasm for joining the local food scene. They want to open a comfortable, friendly pub you can go to for drinks with your pals or meet up for dinner and enjoy yourself safely. It's as simple and as complicated as that.

Elsewhere along this grand stretch of Glasgow's West End at Kelvinbridge you can find cakes and coffee at the colourful Cake Bar by Three Sisters Bake, old school pints at The Belle, views over the river and an IPA at Inn Deep, Glasgow's most popular pizza at Paesano, epic churros at Loop and Scoop, alongside refined dining at Cail Bruich or bánh mì sandwiches from Non Viet. Roots & Fruits is your local florist,

Cake Bar by Three Sister Bake

organic food, fruit and veg store and deli.

Blair and Sheridan jewellers enjoy an excellent reputation for artistry in their design workshop crafting bespoke engagement rings and more intricate pieces. Meanwhile, sisters Eleanor, Charlotte and Elizabeth Paulin have quickly built Paulin Watches into a strong Glasgow brand from their shop on Great Western Road.

Further up the road, many strands of life come together at Bananamoon. There's plenty of space and light, quirky design and art motifs in this wee neighbourhood hangout. They are as comfortable serving you a cheese and beans toastie as they are offering a Levantine flatbread spinach manakish pizza. A mezzanine level will soon be a speakeasy style upstairs bar area.

Tables are populated by students, families, folk taking a break while walking their dogs. There's outside tables that catch the sun late into the evening. The menu is made up of different Middle Eastern plates, featuring family recipes, principally from the owner's mum and granny.

They have also inspired the Mrs Falafel food truck *(above)*, a brand new part of the business – think fully loaded pittas, wraps, lots of babaganoush and lamb koftas. You'll find Mrs Falafel on Ashley Street in Woodlands.

Faces of Glasgow

Meet some of the people who make Glasgow an interesting place to live and shape our perception of the city.

Portraits by Brian Sweeney.

⊙ sweeneypix

Gavin Mitchell

Looking back at Still Game, Gavin agrees that they unintentionally captured a particular point in time for Glasgow. "I walk around a lot of the areas we filmed in when I'm out with my dog, Bob, and you can see all the changes. We are all still amazed at the genuine warmth in the reaction to the show".

More recently, he appeared in a production of Casablanca for A Play, A Pie and a Pint at the Oran Mor: "I've missed their lunchtime shows during lockdown. It's the essence of what theatre should be - cheap, accessible and it brings people together. They give opportunities to young actors and writers, you have old hands involved. We all get together and figure out a production fairly quickly, it is exciting and a bit scary. All of a sudden you're out there on that wee stage. The smell of pies, and you're away."

🌐 playpiepint.com

Sacred Paws

Rachel Aggs and Eilidh Rodgers met in indie pop group Golden Grrrls before recording their own debut EP.

"We started off long distance, travelling back and forth to London, where Rachel lived.

"Now, we're neighbours on the Southside, it's a lot easier and there's lots of low key places on Victoria Road to hang out when we are not playing music" Eilidh says.

"At the moment, as we're not touring, it feels good to start building that sense of community, a sense of place," adds Rachel; "Glasgow is a place I feel very comfortable making music and it is good to know that when we do eventually go off on tour, that this is where we will be coming back to."

As well as performing at Celtic Connections Festival and sessions for BBC 6 Music, Sacred Paws won the Scottish Album of the Year Award in 2017 with their first full-length album *Strike a Match*.

Their most recent album was last year's *Run Around the Sun*.

⊕ **sacredpaws.co.uk**

barry crerar

Independent film production company barry crerar was set up by Rosie Crerar and Ciara Barry in 2016 with the support of a BFI Vision Award.

"At the time we started, we were thinking about where the Scottish new wave of film is going to come from, considering we are so vibrant in theatre, art and music.

"We decided to set up a production company that would capture the modern Glasgow that we know in short films and features" Rosie says.

They work with filmmakers and screenwriters from their base at Film City, the studio and office space housed within a redeveloped Govan Town Hall.

"We want writers to be able to tell authentic stories on screen that originated in Scotland" Ciara says.

🌐 **barrycrerar.com**

Harry Olorunda and Zandra Yeaman

Zandra has worked for the Coalition for Racial Equality and Rights to co-ordinate Scotland's Black History Month, which has taken place during October since 2001, and draws on the stories of African, Caribbean and Asian people who often have a direct link with this country through slavery, colonialism and migration. She was recently appointed Curator of Discomfort at The Hunterian Museum, University of Glasgow, with the challenge of finding new, inclusive ways of interpreting collections that may be contested and are sensitive to different viewpoints.

She is passing on her role with Black History Month to Harry. "It's important that us older activists recognise that young people are coming through to take this work forward and that we must work across communities and generations to build a bridge of trust to bear the weight of the truth we are trying to deliver."

Harry works in the drinks industry and lives in the West End. As he takes up his new role he says: "There's a lot of activism in the city and I want to help bring people together and give them confidence and the opportunity to shine."

🌐 blackhistorymonthscotland.org

Simon Murphy

Simon Murphy is a lecturer
at Glasgow Kelvin College
and a former photographer
for The Herald. Over the last
20 years he has undertaken a
photographic project to capture
the neighbourhood of Govanhill
through pictures of the people
who live and work there.

When lockdown cancelled an
exhibition of the images at Street
Level Photoworks, he instead
put the prints in the windows of
the neighbourhood shops and
restaurants so the community
could see them.

"People respond to the project
through a sense of nostalgia I
think, it might be for a few years
ago or a few weeks ago. The
changes happen quickly in a small
area. There's always something
happening and folk out on the
street so that's what I capture.

"Govanhill will continue to be a
character in my work, it's what I
know, it's where my dad was from
and where I grew up. The project
will go on."

🌐 simonmurphyphotographer.com

Last Night From Glasgow

A patron-funded not-for-profit record label, their name is taken from the line "When I called you last night from Glasgow" in ABBA's *Super Trouper*.

Their focus is on ensuring artists have a fair deal and financing to record music while reinvesting any profits in new records.

"It's being promoted on the principle of socialism" founder Ian Smith says, pictured here with wife Julia.

"I wanted to do something where those that have can come together to help those that don't have. My granny used to say, if you can help people, then you should.

"I love music and we are working to make the industry better."

Artists who have released music on the label include Bis, TeenCanteen and Mark W. Georgsson.

LNFG have 18 LPs planned for release in 2021.

🌐 lastnightfromglasgow.com

Fraser Taylor

Fraser studied Printed Textiles at Glasgow School of Art before leaving for the bright lights of London in 1981 and then a job as a visiting professor at the Art Institute of Chicago.

He returned home three years ago, taking up a studio at The Briggait and he says he couldn't be happier to be back: "The city was always in my head while I was away. I felt the familiarity when I returned but there was so much unknown as well. Already I've been encouraged to see new things and meet new people. When I was at the Art School in the late 70s, Glasgow was all about interactions.

"I like walking along the Clyde from Partick to Glasgow Green and looking at the city. I carry a sketchbook all the time. It is a view that never gets boring."

⊕ **waspsstudios.org.uk/ creatives/fraser-taylor**

73

Cobolt Collective

A mural art group founded by Erin Bradley-Scott, Chelsea Frew, Kat Loudon and Edda Karólína Ævarsdóttir.

They were working in studio space at SWG3 when they decided to form an all-female team of street artists.

One of their biggest works is a mural on Brown Street, close to the Broomielaw that was commissioned to celebrate the 30 year anniversary of Glasgow's Doors Open Days Festival.

It features depictions of local landmarks and two lines from a Liz Lochhead poem, The Bargain.

"Yes today we're in love aren't we? with the whole splintering city"

Edda says: "We wanted to change the direction of mural art in Glasgow and get more women involved. We hope to inspire people to get out and paint. Our aim is to spread a positive, bold and bright message."

⊙ **coboltcollective**

Baldvin Ringsted and Ragnar Jónasson

Baldvin and Ragnar are both Icelandic artists who met and became friends while studying in Glasgow 14 years ago. They have studio space at the Whisky Bond building, seen here in the background.

A repurposed warehouse, it is home to a community of designers, makers and creative businesses alongside the Glasgow Sculpture Studios and production workshops for wood, metal, plaster and ceramics.

The ground floor cafe, operated by Piece, will make you one of the best sandwiches in the city.

Baldvin has a musical background and works across collage, sculpture, painting, installations, and video.

Ragnar is a painter who also works with sculpture and photography, depending on the idea. Both have worked with visual artist Jim Lambie and have hosted exhibitions in local galleries.

Ragnar says "After you have been here for a while, you feel a great sense of community, and that we're all connected. You don't have to go far to find other artists."

⊕ **baldvinringsted.com**

⊕ **glasgowsculpturestudios.org/ ragnar-jonasson**

Harri and Jasper James

Jasper James grew up surrounded by records. He learned to DJ at 13 and made his debut at the Sub Club, joining the family business and playing back to back with his dad Harri.

One of Resident Advisor's Top 100, he launched his own label, Mitchell Street Records, after releasing music on Optimo Trax and Glasgow Underground.

Harri started off as a DJ in the 1980s before creating Subculture with Domenic Cappello, the Sub Club's Saturday night and the longest running weekly house music event in the country.

"What keeps it exciting for us, Dom and I, is that we're always trying to discover new music and we can then try and squeeze as many of those new ones into our sets as we can."

Apart from Sub Club, Harri's Best of Glasgow recommendations include The Berkeley Suite, The Admiral, Chinaskis,The Belle, Kelvingrove Cafe and Julie's Kopitiam.

☁ djjasperjames

🅕 HarriAndDomenic

Gene Kelly, Central Station. 1953

Sophia Loren, 1982

The Empire Exhibition at Bellahouston Park, 1938

Elizabeth Taylor, heading to Rogano, 1979

Mae West visits Glasgow, 1947

Rush hour on Jamaica Bridge, 1962

Launch of Ton Ruahine, built for New Zealand at John Brown Shipyards In Clydebank, 1950

Times Past

The Herald, the longest running national newspaper in the world, has been documenting the life of the city since 1783. It was joined in this endeavour by what became the **Glasgow Times** in 1876.

Over the course of generations, photographers and reporters were there to capture exciting events, the arrival of Hollywood stars, family successes and neighbourhood struggles.

These local stories deserve to be told, and every week, the *Times Past* section of the Glasgow Times looks back at some of these moments.

The Herald   **Glasgow** Evening **Times**

Spring sunshine, Bridgeton Cross, 1967

ty Springfield at tral Hotel, 1964

Ladies of the Glasgow Keep Fit Movement, 1939

81

PJ MOORE IS VERY EASY TO talk to. We are gabbing away while wandering across from the Kelvingrove to the nearby Ronzio cafe to pick up takeaway teas. I've never met him before, but we have a friend in common – Irish journalist Ken Sweeney. Ken made a radio documentary, *In Search of The Blue Nile*, about the musical journey of PJ, Robert Bell and Paul Buchanan. The recording was inspired by a trip Ken made to Glasgow, where he was keen to explore a cityscape that he had imagined through the albums he had listened to while growing up.

He wanted to see the places connected to the music. The show was broadcast on RTÉ Radio, found an audience around the world and was then picked up by BBC Radio Scotland.

We take a walk back and sit on the steps of the museum. The tall tenements of Argyle Street and the elegant turrets of Kelvin Hall look vivid in the afternoon sunshine. Skateboarders are improvising a circuit in the garden and you can see activity along the mini-canyon of Regent Moray Street.

I mention the documentary and the connection Ken made with Glasgow through music. At times, Blue Nile songs can seem a bit too ethereal to be written about Sauchiehall Street or Byres Road in the 1980s, yet *Tinseltown in the Rain* is still about us: "It's there to be immutable. *Tinseltown* will never change. I mean the structure of the song, not the poetry. It's written in stone."

PJ thinks their debut, 1984's *A Walk Across the Rooftops*, has the most Glasgow in it: "The second record (Hats) has more of actual America in it because by then we'd had a short US promotional visit

The downtown lights shine on. PJ Moore reflects on a musical and personal connection to Glasgow.

Words: Paul Trainer

in search of the Blue Nile

for Rooftops. The first record's a more naive imaging of Glasgow as an American city and it's vertical and black and white. Hats is techicolour and more horizontal, but the first one's a fearless leap in the dark, and I love it for that."

This makes me think about the point when Glasgow moved from a sepia tone, post-industrial city, into a brighter modern era as a place for artists and musicians to find their voice. Before I get lost in metaphors, PJ continues: "We cut off London when we were making the records, it was all independent. The music doesn't sound as if it was made using lo-fi equipment. It's funny. People talk about polish and smoothness and beauty but I was working as a waiter at the time, we were borrowing synths and the box that I used to interface with the studio, that enabled us to take the first step, cost five pounds."

The European City of Culture year in 1990 was a breakthrough in how Glasgow perceived itself. The Blue Nile were back home after touring and the Royal Concert Hall was due to open so they found

A Walk Across the Rooftops, The Blue Nile's first album.

themselves being asked to play the first concert at the new venue – "but by then Glasgow was already a hotspot for pop, I'll give you my theory on that if you want?". I do.

"Well, in a place like London. The size of it, it's hard for people to find the scene, you'd have a few venues for punk, whatever's happening, they're there. Good bands and bad ones. Then the New Romantics had places, Boy George at the Blitz Club, Spandau Ballet. But in the absence of that, everyone in London's just walking around going, "Anybody know a bass player, and what kind of bassline should he play anyway?" And it was at that point these A&R guys with their bomber jackets and their attache cases started jumping on the shuttle and coming to Glasgow, where they knew they could at least find something."

I ask Paul where he was waitering in the early days of the band: "Nico's, Rock Garden. The Ultratheque. It was a great laugh, man. Nico's was set up as a cocktail bar and art students loved going there, but what they didn't like to do was spend money on Harvey Wallbangers or Brandy Alexander or whatever passed for class at the time. But you could get a coffee or a beer, and that was a first.

PJ Moore on Gibson Street.

These places were important for cultural exchange too. It's where you could go in and meet someone with a funny haircut and you might end up getting a gig out of it." At the same time he was running a rehearsal studio, "below a very dodgy second-hand shop at The Barras." Things changed when "we saw a chance, the idea to send messages from here in music, realistically."

PJ made a downloadable walking tour that includes the Download landmarks associated with the band. Locatify Smartguide on App Store then search for Glasgow. *A Walk Across the Rooftops* was recorded in a flat in Otago Street: "the building was like a member of the band".

Then there was a one-bedroom bedsit on Buckingham Terrace: "It came to me through a friend who knew I was looking for a place in Glasgow. I was renting in Edinburgh – Paul visited once and we did *From a Late Night Train* – but it was time to get out of there. I moved in, we'd meet tape recorder in the middle of the room, watching the traffic pass: "Headlights on the Parade." We made half of Hats like that. We'd take a break and go a walk to the Cul de Sac bar on Ashton Lane".

We talk more about the sense of place in the music. This side of town is where the band met and have the strongest connection he thinks: "The West End's almost a city on its own. We were all from the Northside, but the uni brings you here, even if you're back staying with your maw, you're heading for Byres Road." But are we listening to a more cinematic version of the city than where they were living? "We always felt American. Everyone grew up watching American movies four times a week when they were kids. We were applying that dream for ourselves more than anybody else. No-one looked at Hope Street and said it was like Madison Avenue, right? There was something in those vistas for me, I've got notebooks, I was trying to draw a big long street with exactly that kind of vibe, that's Easter Parade. The Glasgow you see now, it isn't the Glasgow that was there when we were writing the songs. It never existed. It was part Chicago, part New York, part Brigadoon."

GLASGOW LIFE

Sound of the City

Paul English takes a look at the local music scene and finds the connections between Glasgow venues and bands.

'RODDY FRAME WAS THE first act to play Glasgow's ABC and described the main hall there as big enough to feel important and small enough to feel intimate," says Glasgow music guide Fiona Shepherd, "I think you can apply that to Glasgow in general."

As with many of his songs, the Aztec Camera frontman's words landed perfectly on the absolute truth.

Glasgow is a big city in a small country, whose musical impact echoes around the world. It was the first city in Britain to be awarded UNESCO City of Music status, in 2008.

The award was an acknowledgment of the significant history and vibrancy of its musical landscape. Of course, this recognition was something the place already knew. No-one who lived in Glasgow needed a governmental organisation to tell them. Anyone who ever spent a night in a Barrowlands audience, invariably left with something far richer than anything bestowed by the United Nations.

Glasgow's music scene is as integral to its life force now as the yards and trading houses of its storied industrial history.

Its venues, both those consigned to memory and those whose lights remain lit today, are laden with

Bay City Rollers fans at the Apollo in 1973

The venue of dreams, Barrowland Ballroom

City Tours, a variety of walks which reveal the city's past glories, built heritage and contemporary successes.

"Once we established the tours, we discovered very quickly that the way to tell people the story of Glasgow's music, is to do it through the venues," she says, nodding at the "tall tales" of the city's legendary Apollo, where rambunctious audiences made the balcony bounce. No act who played on its stage ever forgot the Glasgow Apollo.

Today, the venues are very different, but the passion remains. The vast 12,000 capacity Hydro on the banks of the Clyde was the second busiest venue in the world in 2019, behind London's O2. But the story of the city's music owes as much to formative influential snugs like King Tut's Wah Wah

lutely vital to the music history of Glasgow. If you're talking about popular music in Glasgow around the turn of the century then you don't get much more popular than Harry Lauder," she says, recalling the vaudeville star, who at one time was the highest-paid performer in the world.

Glasgow's modern cultural renaissance can be traced back to 1990 when the city, struggling under Conservative government strategy of deindustrialisation, was crowned European City of Culture.

As a 14-year-old living in a Renfrewshire suburb waiting for somewhere to go, the city's lights and promise, sparkling in the rain, were hugely enticing.

While my forebears saw out the end days of industrial toil, I grew towards a place whose cultural reinvigoration would come to offer

'No act who played on its stage ever forgot the Glasgow Apollo'

lore.

Its audiences are venerated by acts who come from all around to play for them.

And the lives the city's folk lead have generated words, sentiments and songs which resonate in the hearts of millions well beyond the city's limits.

How best to illustrate the import of its legacy than with the reminder that skiffle singer Lonnie Donegan was born in Bridgeton, in the city's east end, in 1931.

And, as George Harrison himself put it, "Without Lonnie Donegan, there would have been no Beatles."

Music writer Fiona Shepherd helps run the Glasgow Music

Hut, The Hug and Pint, 13th Note, Mono, Stereo and The Glad Cafe. Together all its live spaces float a cultural scene with an estimated annual worth of £160 million.

Of course, the richest measurement of its impact lies beyond its effect on contemporary finance. Shepherd's tours include a visit to The Panopticon on the city's Trongate, an authentically preserved 1800s music hall known for its ribald audiences and celebrated as the venue where Stan Laurel made his debut.

"It's a big highlight on the tour, people often aren't expecting it. But it's abso-

abundant privilege. Three years after the City of Culture I moved to Glasgow to study, and have enjoyed living and working in the legacy of its reinvention ever since.

"The Arches, the Royal Concert Hall and King Tut's all emerged that year," says Shepherd. "There was a cultural confidence and a shaking off of the 'No Mean City' image. The idea of Glasgow as a cosmopolitan city took root at that point."

Canadian-born academic Dr Matt Brennan is the co-author of *The History of Live Music in Britain 1968-1984: From Hyde Park to the Haçienda.*

"There's a wonderful range of venue size, which isn't true of every city," says the University of Glasgow reader in popular music. "It means an act can build their fanbase. We've maybe even been spoiled for choice with venues.

"It adds to the character of the

Hands up at Sub Club

iour beloved both to bands and audience in the city's most famous venue.

"I saw DJ Shadow at the Barrowlands in 2002. I wasn't expecting people to be stage diving, but they were. And I remember how the crowd stamped their feet to bring him back out on that wonderful Barrowland ballroom floor," he says.

Stadium fillers CHVRCHES (right),

city, from a music-making perspective. Glasgow is a place where musicians from across Scotland and the wider UK move to. There are lots of opportunities.

"It's one of those nicely-sized cities, big enough to have a vibrant and diverse music-making culture, but small enough that if you're participating in that culture, you're likely to bump into people again and again, build networks and friendships."

It has proved a successful game plan time and again.

The Postcards Records scene in the late 70s and early 80s delivered era-defining and hugely influential acts like Orange Juice, Josef K and The Go-Betweens, forging a path which bands like The Delgados and Mogwai would follow with their own labels Rock Action and Chemikal Underground.

The mid 80s and early 90s saw high-sheen success for mainstream acts like Simple Minds, Deacon Blue and Del Amitri. At the same time, Glasgow's alternative music landscape was producing bands like The Pastels, Belle and Sebastian, Mogwai, The Vaselines,

Primal Scream's Bobby Gillespie in full flow

with the likes of Primal Scream, Travis and Franz Ferdinand getting their rocks off at the top of the charts.

At the time of writing, the work of electronic acts like DJ and producer Hudson Mohawke and electro-pop conquerors CHVRCHES are spilling across continents, their sound connecting millions to the influences of formative nights spent immersed in the clubs like Sub Club and the much-missed Arches.

And, who can forget, these streets also delivered Lulu and Donovan to the wider world.

"From the late 1970s onwards, there hasn't really been a fallow period," says Brennan. "Glasgow has always been a city that has produced acts that have been influential, whether it's at a subcutural underground level or chart-toppers."

Brennan has lived in Glasgow for almost 20 years, long enough to understand its quirks while still seeing them with a visitor's perspective.

Perfectly placed, perhaps, to consider a definitive behav-

"I'd never heard a sound like it. The crowd knew that the floor could do that. It really says something about the interaction between the audience and the space."

A thrilling noise, arguably more definitive of the city's highest spirits now than the once-fierce Hampden Roar, given the distinctly more successful trajectory of our music scene's fortunes compared to those of our national football team in their Mount Florida home.

It was Dundonian Michael Marra who penned one of the city's most beloved songs, *Mother Glasgow*, a lullaby which captures her characteristics of compassion, toil and unerring hope.

"Let Glasgow flourish," goes the final line, echoing the city motto. It's a sentiment proudly shared over the years by millions who carry this city's sounds in their hearts.

STUART MARTIN

Glasgow Techno

Orde Meikle and Stuart McMillan set up
Soma Records in 1991. They are Slam.

AS SLAM, ORDE MEIKLE
and Stuart McMillan were
at the vanguard of Glas-
gow's underground music
scene in the late 1980s,
then instrumental in the
explosion of the UK techno scene
through the 90s and beyond.

In three decades of exploits
with Soma, they have travelled far
and wide, leaving scorch marks on
dancefloors across the globe. The
independent Glasgow label established its reputation releasing
early work from Jeff Mills, Silicone
Soul's *Right On Right On*, Felix da

Housecat's early track *Clashback*
and the original vinyl version of
Daft Punk's breakthrough single
Da Funk. They continue to provide
an outlet for local talent.

Slam have been instrumental in
the development of the Riverside
Festival with some of the world's
leading DJs and live acts playing
alongside local talent, while Slam
Radio's online broadcasts from
Glasgow have found an enthusiastic international audience, and
their Maximum Pressure club
events at SWG3 are among the best
parties in town.

They spoke to Best of Glasgow
about what it's all about.

Orde Meikle
My interest in music in the first
place was, growing up in the West
End, we were surrounded by
venues for live concerts. The GU at
the university, the QM, the Cotton
Club – Maestro's as it was called
back then. Then you had Tiffany's
and Mayfair and the Apollo. If
someone big was touring and they
were only doing a couple of gigs in

*'It became one of those
scenes. People found it and
they have held onto it'*

the UK, then we'd be pretty sure Glasgow would be included. All kinds of bands – reggae was a big thing for me. Going to see early Simple Minds gigs. I was in a privileged situation for music growing up in Glasgow.

I left the city and I went down south for a couple of years to Sheffield and, you know, experienced the clubs in the North of England and bands, but Glasgow had made such an indelible impression on me, with the plethora of different music you could go out and see on a weekly basis.

I hightailed it back, put it that way. When I got the chance to come back to Glasgow, culturally, you know, the whole bar scene and the restaurants and style, and just everything was better here than anything I'd seen. It was all going on.

I think Glasgow has its own little scenes and people stick to them. I don't mean we are shuttered or blinkered, we just don't swing widely through styles of music like some other cities. Techno became one of those scenes. People found it and they have held onto it. Jeff Mills pointed out that, when he felt there was a backlash against techno in the late nineties, he was still coming to Glasgow as he could still see the enthusiasm.

The more we have travelled as DJs, there are good scenes everywhere, probably more so in the last decade. But when we first started travelling, it just made you realise how special a place you came from and the nights you get, the levels of energy that you took for granted in Glasgow that didn't seem to exist in too many other places.

When we released *Positive Education* on Soma, people had that song and then they found us. Someone who plays vinyl, you look at the label, around the centre spin would be some information on where the label

Clap your hands: Slam and the crowd at the Riverside Festival

Daft Punk

was based. We started receiving CDs and mixes from Uzbekistan and Hong Kong. We weren't that far into what is now a reasonably lengthy history of Soma and people were hearing us and identifying with the music on the other side of the world, and I think that's quite cool. It was unexpected to be honest. I continue to be pleasantly surprised by that even now.

Choosing the music we put out, we're always looking for something new. You asked about Daft Punk and we heard *Da Funk* for the first time played off a cassette on a ghetto blaster in a small attic flat in Paris, we instantly knew, you could tell it was special. It had its own sound that was jumping out the speakers.

We put out music that we like at Soma, it's never about commercial success. It's important that people make music for the love of it and

because they believe in it. I think, in Glasgow there's so many influences and everyone has their own interpretation of the music they want to hear but it is a supportive scene. Everyone wants everyone else to do well.

There's a lot of cooperation and you might meet folk who can do artwork for a record or make a video and that's how things thrive.

Glasgow enjoys a very good reputation, especially within nightclub and dance music circles. You know you're going to have a good weekend if you come to Glasgow, it's not going to be wasted money.

I love being on the Subway and going into town. I always remember that folk always say to look up in Glasgow because that's what makes the city special, the buildings and views. I feel like Glasgow has a hopeful outlook, that it's always trying to be better than it was yesterday.

'I feel like Glasgow has a hopeful outlook, that it's always trying to be better than it was yesterday.'

Stuart McMillan

Things didn't really take off for us straight away. We started dabbling in different forms of dance, there was some punk stuff or disco, but that was all 15 years old by the time we were playing it. The thing about the Chicago and Detroit music was it was new. You were separated in a way, because you were from Glasgow and the world was a lot bigger back then. Your main insight into this music was the aesthetic of the record itself and the way the music sounded. At that stage it sounds like music from another planet. It was quite rudimentary, a lot of it was made in people's bedrooms. That had a massive appeal to me. I grew up with punk, so I like that raw element.

We'd been collecting that music for a while before things took off. We were in a good position to be able to play those records and we had a guy that was working with us at the time who was doing really quite provocative artwork. We were doing places like Tin Pan Alley when nobody would go there, it was like everybody had an established Saturday night thing. We had to go outside of that and find places in Glasgow, do our own lighting and projections, put banners up. It grew from there.

We've brought people along

with us through the years, but it's never been our philosophy to be a retro night. I guess we were bitten by the bug of music sounding fresh and the impact of music. The reason we have been about and are still doing stuff is we are never satisfied just doing the same things. We keep moving forward.

Frankie Knuckles, the "Godfather of House"

We started a radio podcast, partly because at that time there wasn't one focusing on techno. We were buying a lot of music and we wanted to showcase what we were playing in the clubs. With the label, we have our ear to the ground and pick up music that excites us. We try to unconsciously set trends rather than follow them.

I think Glasgow is very much part of what makes us do what we do – the scene and running events here. The people we know. It's dif-

ferent. Why would I want to go to Berlin when we've got Glasgow? I know, we've got some draconian licensing laws, but the people, the energy in the clubs, all those things. It makes Glasgow a great place to run parties and to get inspiration.

It's not that big, Glasgow. It's quite a small city. But it punches above its weight with creativity. I think that's it. What that does is, it gives you the opportunity to mingle with people and you get contacts. It almost forces people to work together and collaborate.

Because it is small. Because there's loads of people with that creative energy, they're going to meet more people and ideas become something.

I'm in Anniesland now, look at that as my favourite part of the city. During lockdown, I've been walking everywhere. I've been walking the canal, all the way down to Spiers Wharf which I hadn't been to for years. I go to Finnieston too, it's like what Byres Road once was. I was on the Southside recently, on Vicky Road, and it's emerging there and looking like loads of really cool places are opening. You know that way when you have been to some place for about five years and then you go and you're like, "Wow, this is magic."
◎ *slam_djs* ⊕ *slam-djs.com*

My Glasgow: Alan McGee

"The best thing about Glasgow is the music scene. When I was a little boy I used to love going to The Apollo and now I like Barrowlands. I was born in Govanhill and went to school in Mount Florida so I am a Southsider. I like the Malmaison hotel on West George Street for meetings. I like the fish and chip shops here. It's the best dish in Glasgow. Unlike some other places, we have great people and great music."

Trainspotting actor Ewen Bremner will play Glasgow music manager Alan McGee in *Creation Stories*, a biopic written by

Dean Cavanagh and Irvine Welsh with Danny Boyle as executive producer. The movie chronicles Creation Records, home to acts such as Primal Scream and Teenage Fanclub from 1983l until its end in 1999.

The film includes scenes based on McGee's early management of The Jesus and Mary Chain, his friendship with Primal Scream singer Bobby Gillespie and the moment he signed Oasis after seeing them perform at King Tut's Wah Wah Hut in 1993.

You can listen to Alan McGee's show on
⊕ *boogalooradio.com*

Soundtrack
of the
Streets

FROM SOLEMN LONE PIPERS TO FOUR-piece rock bands giving it laldy, Glasgow's music scene is a popular and prominent part of the city's street culture.

It's a proving ground for musical performers aiming to be the next breakthrough artist, like Twin Atlantic or Gerry Cinnamon. There's a competitive market in Lewis Capaldi cover versions.

You will soon notice well-established pitches along Buchanan Street and Argyle Street for street performers.

Drum and pipe band Clanadonia, rock band The Best Bad Influence (left) and singer Rach Songbird are regulars along Sauchiehall Street. A brief interaction with their enthusiastic, entertaining presence will leave you remembering an old tune or humming along to a new one. Crowds often linger to join in.

The Best Bad Influence say: "We would play anywhere, but it's exciting when it's in Glasgow. You get to meet all sorts of characters."

f *buskersofglasgow*
Words: Islay Raimund

Glasgow's own gin
THE GLASGOW DISTILLERY: MAKAR GIN
📍 Deanside Road, G52 4XB 📞 0141 404 7191
🌐 glasgowdistillery.com

The first gin to be distilled in the city of Glasgow, Makar Original is a bold, vibrant, juniper-led gin that derives its name from the Scots word for a poet. Distilled by hand in small batches within their copper pot still, Annie at their Hillington headquarters. Tours aren't running at the moment but will return when relaxation of restrictions permit. In the meantime, the team are running weekly whisky tastings online, an opportunity to learn more about 1770 Single Malt Scotch Whisky.

They have introduced the distinctive and delicious Makar Oak Aged Gin which brings in rich spicy notes gained from ageing in new European oak casks. Soft on the nose and lively on the palate; perfectly paired with ginger ale over ice for a refreshing gin and ginger. You can get two free Fever Tree Ginger Ales with every bottle of Makar Oak Aged Gin you order direct from the distillery website. Their Banditti Club spiced rum can be spotted behind the bar at many of the city's leading music venues.

Makar Gin

TASTE OF GLASGOW

Something for the weekend with food and drink to enjoy at home

Roll Shop
COMET PIECES
📍 150 Queen Margaret Dr, G20 8NY 📞 0141 945 2135
🌐 cometpieces.co.uk

The name is inspired by the PS Comet: a paddle steamer launched on the Clyde in 1812, commemorated by a large painting in the cafe. Their bacon is from Ramsay's of Carluke. Papercup supply the coffee. Teas are by The Wee Tea Company. Fruit and veg is from Locavore. Oh, and the wood for the

furniture is from GalGael in Govan. But you are really here for a Mortons roll layered up with extravagant toppings. Try steak lorne sausage with haggis, onions, potato scone, poached egg and Tapatio hot sauce. A high-concept roll shop.

Healthy food delivery
THE HONEST CHEF
🌐 honestchef.co.uk

New businesses have developed during lockdown, hospitality has had to adapt and some concepts have been put on pause for now. Chef John Traynor organised regular pop-up dining events at interesting locations. His new concept is a meal preparation and delivery service, a team up with award winning butcher Tom Rogers.

All our meals have no added salt/refined sugar & no artificial flavours or preserv-

atives. "Giving back to the community is important to us. That's why with help from folk purchasing deliveries we will be donating a minimum of 50 fresh meals every week to Glasgow food banks and community food projects. So everyone will have the opportunity to access wholesome, nutritious meals" John explains.

Cocktail Delivery
BOTTLE DROP
🌐 bottle-drop.co.uk

For those looking for a way to bring the bar to your own home, online off-sale website Bottle Drop offers a home delivery service across Glasgow. Their range includes small independent brands from the West of Scotland, IPAs, specialist craft beer and in-house fresh cocktails, bottled and transported to enjoy at home.

Finding Glasgow

FOOD HISTORIAN AND editor Ben Mervis arrived in Glasgow to study for a year. Eleven years later, he's still here. After graduating from university, Ben worked at Noma in Copenhagen as an assistant to the head chef, gaining experience in the food world.

He returned to his new home to launch a magazine. *Fare* is a bi-annual publication that explores city culture through the intersection of food, history and community. Ben has gone on to be a contributor to the Netflix's food documentary series *Chef's Table* and is currently writing a cookbook from the Southside. This is his local story.

"I was a student at a university outside Philadelphia, which is where I'm from. I remember wanting to study abroad, and there was this exciting option to come to Scotland. I had travelled Europe in my teenage years, but I didn't know much about the place. I won a scholarship and that was it. I showed up at this perfect stage in my life, where I needed a new proving ground. Somewhere to create that blank slate.

Fare's Glasgow edition, with a cover image at The Laurieston.

I remember the first time I saw Glasgow. Flying over Scotland, early in the morning, the green hills, then coming into land, seeing the fog, and cars cutting through it. I showed up at halls, then walked around for about three hours trying to find town. I met my flatmates and within a couple of weeks, I was living as if Glasgow was my city, and I had lived there forever. I never felt like an outsider. Even though I was clearly a foreigner, I felt included.

The West End for me now, it's connected to those student days. I turn every corner and think about the friends I made or some of the parties I went to in flats.

The memories can be a bit intense sometimes. I realised I wanted to explore a new place in the city so I moved to Pollokshields and now I'm in Govanhill. It's a nice area to live in, you're close to huge parks, it's fairly affordable to rent or buy a home and to start up your own business.

If I want to show off Glasgow to visitors then I usually start off with a bacon roll in an older cafe, then a walk through Pollok Park to see all the Highland cows, then a visit to Pollok House. I'm looking forward to the Burrell Collection reopening, I think it is possibly the finest collection in the city and the building is really beautiful. Then an Indian restaurant for dinner, then I would take them to the pub. Probably a series of pubs.

My Holy Trinity of Glasgow Indian food at the moment is Mother India, probably the upstairs one on Westminster Terrace, Ranjit's Kitchen on Pollokshaws Road, and the new one on my list is Kebabish, which I only went to for the first time recently. That is one of my locals too – I thought it was absolutely fantastic, and I was so excited that it's a five minute walk from my house. In terms of bars, my two favourites are The Lauriston and the Star Bar – they used to do an excellent karaoke night. I have a very soft spot for Nice N' Sleazy in town from my Uni days. The Hielan Jessie is a great pub, and it's so cheap.

Right now, I'm subletting a place in Partick while I'm renovating my flat. I'm not far from KAF, and I'm going there all the time to pick up bread. KAF is wonderful. I really love a new bakery at the end of my street in Govanhill called Flower. That is a young couple, who've just done a sort of DIY operation. I could talk about bakeries and cakes all day.

When I published the Glasgow edition of *Fare*, there were lots of little stories that I wanted to include. I attempted to put together a pretty well-rounded magazine that showed what it's like to live here. I wanted people to get a sense of what I'd found here. I've a real enthusiasm for this city. I count it as a blessing that I turned up in Glasgow.
You can order the Glasgow edition of Fare at ⊕ faremag.com

SAM A HARRIS

'Within a couple of weeks, I was living as if Glasgow was my city, and I had lived there forever. I never felt like an outsider...'

Distillery Tour
CLYDESIDE DISTILLERY

📍 100 Stobcross Road, G3 8QQ 📞 0141 212 1401
🌐 theclydeside.com

The Clydeside Distillery opened to visitors in 2017, following the production of its first spirit. Whisky is produced by the river, in an old Pump House building which was built

ASHLEY COOMBES

in 1877 on the Queen's Dock, close to the Riverside Museum. They offer interactive whisky tours, alongside a whisky shop and café. Make your way through the history of whisky, brought to life by film, pictures and words, as part of self-led or guided tours before visiting their tasting room.

New York Style Pizza
ERROL'S HOT PIZZA

📍 379 Victoria Road, G42 8RZ 📞 0141 423 0559
📷 errolshotpizzashop

A tiny place, they opened with little fanfare and quickly attracted attention for a selection of New York style pizzas. Thick crusts, crispy base, wide slices for folding, bubbling cheese and a sprinkling of toppings. Exceptional results. There's a bit of a dive bar style to Errol's, with odd artwork arranged on dark walls and a buzzy nighttime vibe. "Walk-ins only, takeaway when possible". The pizza chefs were previously at Alchemilla so they know about balancing flavours. They all live locally and decided to create the kind of evening place they would like to hangout. There are some interesting small plates on the menu featuring broccoli, chilli, artichokes, garlic and lemon.

Take our recommendations as you explore the local hospitality scene.

Burritos
RAFA'S

📍 1103 The Hidden Lane, Argyle Street, G3 8ND
🌐 rafasdiner.com

Rafa's, a wee Arizona-style Mexican diner opened on The Hidden Lane in Finnieston in September and has already attracted an enthusiastic following. Carnitas, burritos, tortillas, lots of hot sauce.

Deep Dish Pizza
THUNDERCAT PUB & DINER

📍 84 Miller Street, G1 1DT, 0141 221 1568
🌐 thundercatpubdiner.co.uk

A new arrival on Miller Street, where SoHo pizza once was, Thundercat Pub + Diner is the reason you now see so many Chicago style deep dish pizzas lathered in tomato sauce on your Glasgow Instagram

feed. Their fried chicken and waffles have also captured the imagination. From the team behind Buck's Bar with Yvonne Noon, formerly of The Sisters restaurant, in the kitchen.

Bourbon Bar
VAN WINKLE

📍 94 Byres Road, G12 8TB 📞 0141 339 9993
🌐 vanwinkle.co.uk

Van Winkle started out as a bourbon bar opposite the Barrowland Ballroom at the Gallowgate, before a second branch opened on Byres Road, taking over the corner previously occupied by The Hill. They have more than 50 bourbons to choose from alongside American whiskeys, cocktails, beers and wine. You'll also find an excellent five cheese macaroni, Buffalo chicken wings, burgers, sandwiches and bar snacks. Van Winkle also has a dog-friendly menu, developed by BBC Scotland's resident vet Ross Allan from Pets'n'Vets.

French Breakfast
LE PETIT COCHON

📍 9 Radnor Street, G3 7UA 📞 0141 357 1666
🌐 *lepetitcochon.co.uk*

Sitting on the edge of Kelvingrove Park, this independent neighbourhood wine bar and bistro transforms local produce and imported treats into strong, seasonal dishes.

A local favourite, they have reopened Wednesday to Sunday with a new head chef. Try crêpes with jambon, gruyére and fried egg for a continental start to the day.

Fishmonger
BERNARD CORRIGAN

📍 184-200 Howard St, G1 4HW 📞 0141 552 4368
🌐 *bernardcorrigan.com*

More than 200 restaurants in Glasgow rely on Bernard Corrigan to deliver their fish and poultry every day. The family firm has been serving restaurants and trade in Scotland since 1949. They have recently adapted to changing times by introducing a home delivery service so you can order the same produce that reaches restaurants directly to your door.

Anarchist Cafe
PINK PEACOCK

🌐 *pinkpeacock.gay*

"Queer-friendly, Yiddish-speaking anarchist café aims to revolutionise Glasgow" proclaimed the Times of Israel. The Jeru-

salem-based newspaper put the spotlight on an emerging business in Govanhill, Pink Peacock. Run by Morgan Holleb and Joe Isaac, the project will see a kosher café open in Glasgow's most ethnically diverse neighbourhood.

The founding principle is to provide "a Jewish space where you can be loudly queer and you're welcome". Customers at the café will be told the break-even price of the food when they order and can then "pay either side of that all the way down to zero" – a concept that say fits with the cafe's anarchist outlook: "Sometimes it means smashing windows, but sometimes it means feeding people for free".

The pair are negotiating a lease and hope to open some time before the end of the year. Pink Peacock has already been hard at work during lockdown from a home kitchen, producing bagels and challah bread for weekly delivery to 40 to 50 Glasgow households in need from all different backgrounds.

When they officially open their doors, there will be vegan, kosher and halal dishes from the Ashkenazi cookbook. The café will also host revolutionary and social lectures. It will be a space for Yiddish learning, including reviving the Scots Yiddish dialect. Holleb told the Times of Israel: "It is important to us that the Yiddish we do isn't just preservation — we want to use and speak Yiddish, and if it is used in Scotland, we will say Scottish words."

New Gastropub
THE DUKE'S UMBRELLA

📍 363 Argyle Street, G2 8LT

A new bar in the city centre set to offer innovative dishes, creative cocktails and drinks in a stylish setting. Due to open by the end of the year, from the team behind Embargo in the West End.

Toastie
BABOS

📍 1117A Pollokshaws Road, G41 3YH
📷 *babosglasgow*

The Southside gets its very own "Toastie Hoose" in the form of new neighbourhood

spot Babos on Pollokshaws Road. Try a mac 'n' cheese with black pudding toasty to get you started. The new menu also has a cheese, ham, spring onion and fried egg version, a spicy mix of cheese, chorizo, jalapenos, roasted red peppers and rocket or salt and chilli chicken with roasted red peppers and sriracha sauce.

Neapolitan Pizza
PAESANO

📍 94 Miller Street, G1 1DT 📞 0141 258 5565
🌐 *paesanopizza.co.uk*

A legend in its own lunchtime. Glasgow's most popular pizza. Paesano has nailed the cool, casual dining aesthetic. Then there's the pizza itself. Straight out of wood-fired

ovens that provide an intense heat of 500 degrees Celsius to convert a pizza base into a pliable, light and tasty platform for all kinds of fresh toppings and transform the cheese into a creamy delight.

Cheesemonger
GEORGE MEWES CHEESE

📍 106 Byres Road, G12 8TB 📞 0141 334 5900
🌐 *georgemewescheese.co.uk*

It's a name that means something. When you see "cheese from George Mewes" on a restaurant menu, consider it a mark of quality. They supply places like One Devonshire Gardens, The Gannet and Crossbasket

Castle around Glasgow; The Kitchin, and Scran & Scallie through in Edinburgh. You can also just pop into their shop and pick up your own selection, along with oatcakes, quinces and other interesting food.

George worked as a chef all over the world before opening on Byres Road. He began to work exclusively with cheese seven years ago and regularly assembles an interesting range from across the British Isles, France, Italy, Spain and Switzerland.

Restaurants often send their staff to the shop to get an education on cheese and to pick up some of the enthusiasm for produce.

Right now, Isle of Mull cheddar is a best seller. The counter boasts a mix of pasteurised and non pasteurised varieties, all with their individual stories and flavour profiles. Ayrshire Dunlop and Barweys cheddar. Old Winchester and Smoked Cuddy's Cave from Northumberland. Killeen made with pasteurised goats' milk, from Galway in Ireland. The best selection you'll find in Glasgow.

Doughnuts
TANTRUM
⚲ 28 Gordon Street, G1 3PU, 0141 248 1552
⊕ tantrumdoughnuts.com

Glasgow has a sweet tooth. It's not a fad or a trend. We are committed. So when Tantrum Doughnuts, the brainchild of husband and wife team Iain and Annika Baillie began

COLIN MEARNS

making pop-up appearances at markets, they attracted a crowd. Then came a shop on Old Dumbarton Road, which opened in December 2015 and has become a firm favourite in the neighbourhood.

For their next trick, Tantrum rolled into

the city centre, with a place on Gordon Street, close to Central Station. Enter and you are greeted by a colourful, outlandish display of fun treats. Brioche doughnuts, hand-made in small batches, then smothered, filled or glazed with home-made custards, fondants, purées, compotes and jams. Their selection changes when new ingredients become available from local suppliers. Our current favourite is tonka bean with orange oil infused glaze. They also serve an excellent cup of coffee.

Being a chef is all Iain has ever wanted to do. The pastry side of the work appealed to him and he had the chance to hone his technical skills when he spent two years at The Fat Duck in Bray. Returning to Glasgow, Iain sought out a job at Ox & Finch, not long after they opened, because he was impressed with their approach to cooking.

He would work there during the day before baking with Annika through the night, as they looked to establish their business. Annika has front-of-house hospitality experience and a keen eye for branding and marketing – one of the reasons Tantrum has such a strong presence on social media. In the early days, pictures of new doughnuts on Instagram acted as a clarion call to attract new devotees.

In January 2018, Tantrum opened a new bakery to support both shops in a converted railway arch in the contemporary SWG3 event space in the West End. Now there's a team of pastry chefs who roll, glaze and fry through the night, "It's very hard work, and can be surprisingly overwhelming at times but at the end of the day, we get to create delicious doughnuts that make people happy and that's one of the best jobs in the world" Iain says.

Ramen
RAMEN DAYO
⚲ 31 Ashton Lane, G12 8SJ ☎ 0141 334 9095
⊕ ramendayo.co

Like many of the the more interesting new arrivals on the Glasgow food scene, Ramen Dayo – it means "This is Ramen" – started as a pop-up, making an eye-catching debut by taking over a covered lane in Gordon Street and converted it into a scene from a Tokyo back-alley, complete with lanterns,

a Yatai cart and Japanese bar snacks. They are now thriving on Ashton Lane.

Hearty bowls of ramen, prepared from scratch with variations on a rich, creamy pork broth with springy noodles, chashu pork belly, marinated kirkurage mushrooms, nori seaweed, egg and spring onions. The New York Times was impressed. There's also gyoza dumplings. imported sake, turntables and curated playlists. Founder Paul Beveridge was inspired by 12 years living in Japan.

Classic Cafe
UNIVERSITY CAFÉ
⚲ 87 Byres Road, G11 5HN ☎ 0141 339 5217

"Haddock, battered and floating, adrift in a sea of mysterious life-giving oil. The accumulated flavours of many magical things, as it bobs like Noah's Ark, bringing life in all its infinite variety." Chef Anthony Bourdain's order at University Cafe while filming for his

Parts Unknown series in 2015: fish and chips with cheese and curry sauce, deep fried haggis and a bottle of Irn Bru.

The University Cafe is a throwback to the first proliferation of local ice cream parlours across the city. The cafe's enduring appeal is down to an idiosyncratic family fusion of Italian and Glaswegian influences held together in a tiny Art Deco room with slim wood-lined booths and bedecked in kitschy nostalgia.

Students have depended on this place for generations. Sliding into places on a bench to order their hangover crushing meals like pie, beans and chips or macaroni and chips or half pizza and chips. Pretty much everything comes with chips. Except maybe the spaghetti bolognese.

Remember: they'll make you a mighty fried breakfast when you need one. Glaswegians of a certain vintage come to the University Cafe to remember date nights of the past or being brought in for a sweet treat as a kid.

While you will find the building blocks of the Glasgow Diet along with swift delivery of cans of ginger or cups of tea when you visit, above all, this is probably the best place in Glasgow to order ice cream. You might want to move straight to dessert.

The ice cream itself is smooth and supersweet. It's a reminder of a carefree past. Owner Carlo Verrecchia makes ice cream to an old family recipe that has been passed down through the generations. It is food to make you feel good and should be enjoyed with abandon. And ribbons of raspberry sauce.

There's a cabinet beside the till that shows the classic menu, many of ice cream dishes have fallen out of fashion. The display is a Glasgow cultural artefact. You can choose from a normal cone, a straight-forward 99 or opt for the formidable twin double 99 cone impossibly piled with vanilla ice-cream.

Then there's the heritage options ranging from a wafer (two scoops of ice-cream sandwiched between two thin wafer slices) up to a double nougat (the same as before but with two generous slabs of chocolate nougat added). The banana split sundae is pretty special.

University Cafe has welcomed generations of Glaswegians happy with a simple, distinctive brand of hospitality that is gloriously dated. We hope they never change.

Pho
NON VIET
📍 536 Sauchiehall Street, G2 3LX 📞 0141 332 2975
🌐 nonviet.co.uk

Pho, the classic Vietnamese fragrant homemade broth, is ideal comfort food for the Glasgow climate. You'll find the city's best example of the dish on Sauchiehall Street. Garnished with spring onion and coriander, served with beansprouts, lemon and fresh chopped chili. Top with fried tofu, shredded chicken or cooked and rare beef. It's good

for what ails you.

Non Viet is casual dining with plenty of room for groups to share a selection of dishes. Ask questions if you don't understand any of the ingredients and be adventurous with your choices. For dessert, it's the fried ice cream with a sprinkle

of condensed milk and crushed peanut, or mango spring roll with creamy coconut sauce for us. Sister restaurant Non Viet Hai is on Great Western Road.

Tram Station Italian
BATTLEFIELD REST
📍 55 Battlefield Road, G42 9JL 📞 0141 636 6955
🌐 battlefieldrest.co.uk

Built as a particularly impressive-looking tram station in 1915, this local landmark fell into a state of disrepair before being rescued through restoration, led by businessman Marco Giannasi. He opened Battlefield Rest, an Italian bistro, here in 1994. The same head chef is still here after

25 years, with Marino Donati leading the team in the kitchen. Remarkable. They enjoy crossing Scottish and Italian flavours. "We made some cannelloni haggis one day and then customers kept ordering it, so that became a signature dish" Marco says. They

buy cured meats and pasta from North Tuscany. Service is prompt and warm, conversation flows as easily as the wine, people relax and take time over their meal.

Date Night
HALLOUMI
📍 697 Pollokshaws Road, G41 2AB 📞 0141 423 6340
🌐 halloumiglasgow.co.uk

Halloumi looks to Athens for inspiration. Greek flavours shine through from the menu, crafted with modern Mediterranean sensibilities. Visit with a date who like to share their food.

This is leisurely, small plate dining, with plenty of opportunities to interrupt your procession of dishes for cocktails or wine. Gyros: difficult to pronounce, easy to eat. A fresh, light, toasted flat bread stuffed with grilled pork, chicken or halloumi. They also find space for tzatziki, and Glasgow salad – a scattering of chips. Unwrap, divide and hoover up. Halloumi fries are a conspicuous and popular signature dish. There's an express lunch menu Monday to Friday. The original Halloumi restaurant is on Hope Street.

Music Venue Lunch
THE WINGED OX
📍 17 Bain St, G40 2JZ 📞 0141 552 8378
🌐 stlukesglasgow.com

The Winged Ox is the food and drink side of the operation at ultra-hip East End venue St Luke's. The stage in the converted church is regularly graced by some of the biggest names on the music scene for gigs. Meanwhile, the kitchen is cooking up its own headliners on a daily basis. Some of our favourites are the brisket burger, fish finger sandwich or Calton kebabs – gourmet offerings with options like soulaki pork, Cajun chicken and Moroccan veg. Elsewhere on the menu, expect lots of American-tinged soul food with a bit of Glaswegian swagger. It's good, honest bar bites, to be shared with friends between rounds of craft beer or bourbon cocktails. The benches on the outside terrace are a suntrap during the summer and booths in the bar are regularly booked out at weekends.

My Glasgow

JEAN JOHANSSON
Television presenter

WHEN I'M WITH friends in Glasgow I love an afternoon in the city centre. These days I like day drinking that starts with a lunch around 2pm then winds up early, around 8pm, when I jump on a train home. My perfect Glasgow day out is lunch in Princes Square then heading over to The Merchant Pride bar at four o'clock to grab a seat for singer Barbara Bryceland who does a set that brings the city to life every Saturday. It's the place to be in Glasgow, it has a mixed crowd of different people and the atmosphere is positive and happy, I love it.

Glasgow Green holds lots of great memories for me. It's my favourite park in the city. I hosted some concerts there during The Commonwealth games back in 2014 and I've partied there many times at Pride and TRNSMT festival. It's also good for a jog when I fancy a run with a friend at a central location.

Nanakusa is a favourite food place of mine. I'm happy to see the work being done on Sauchiehall Street as I think it's sometimes forgotten about, and Nanakusa is a gem from that part of town. The sushi is fresh and tasty, the decor is simple but stylish and the atmosphere is always buzzy.

For drinks and entertainment, I recommend Hutchesons – the 158 Club Lounge downstairs is cosy, dimly lit and cool. The espresso martinis are delicious.

Gordon Street Coffee is perfect to grab a hot drink and a gab with a pal, it's friendly and has good service. I'm always getting on and off trains so it's a good meeting point.

I love the Glasgow Science Centre for a day out with the family. I've been taking my son there since he was small. There's plenty of space to run around, it's very child friendly and now he's at an age where he can begin to understand some of the science and experi ments. We can spend a whole day there.

For shopping, Fraser's will always be a favourite of mine. It's a Glasgow institution housed in the most beautiful building.

The Royal Concert Hall is a fabulous Glasgow building, I love when there are street performers and crowds lounging around outside on a warm day. It sits at the top of Buchanan Street and I love standing and looking all the way down. It's one of my favourite views of the city.

My Glasgow music? There are so many great bands to choose from – Travis, Simple Minds, Primal Scream but I'd have to go for good old Deacon Blue – *Real Gone Kid* is a Glasgow anthem.

My Glasgow heroes: We have so many Glaswegian heroes from Billy Connolly *(below)* to Alex Ferguson but heroes these days are the everyday Glaswegians that make our city the best in

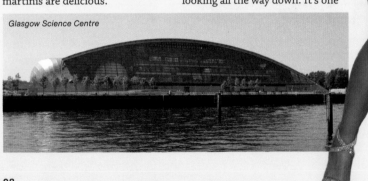

the world from our law enforcement to our to school workers and our brilliant NHS staff, those are the people who make Glasgow.

In terms of parts of the city that are important to me, I love the East End of Glasgow, The Barras, Gallowgate, Dennistoun. It feels historical yet trendy and non-pretentious. It's also very diverse, which I love.

Glasgow Science Centre

The Bakery by Zique

NDEPENDENT BAKERIES ARE opening across the city. Add to that, a new wave of cafes offering their own range of buns, brioche, brownies and other sweet treats and you have one of the city's most exciting food trends.

Cottonrake Bakery on Great Western Road, with a small café attached, keep locals supplied with bread, cakes and sausage rolls. They also serve great coffee. **Honeytrap** is a vegan bakery that's opened at 80 Victoria Road. Ask for their rhubarb almond crumble. **Akara** on Duke Street sells impressive peanut butter dulce de leche brownies. **Sweet Jane Bakehouse**, from the team that brought you Mesa and Cafe Strange Brew, and their range of breads and other bakes is further along the street.

Sugar Fall has eye-catching cakes on Byres Road. Recently, **Root Candy** exchanged collapsible tables at Partick Farmers Market for a new home on Hyndland Street – check out their vegan cookies. The recently opened **Levant Pies** on Park Road is where you will find freshly made baklava, alongside spinach and za'atar bakes or flatbread pizza.

The Bakery by Zique has shelves stocked with freshly baked bread, cakes and savoury bites. There's a new tearoom on Pollokshaws Road, **The Sweet Tart**. For souffle pancakes, **Koko House** is the place. Sustainable bakery and deli, **Zilch**, has opened on Eglinton Street.

Go to **Big Bear Bakery** for your Sunday croissants. The cake stand at **The Hidden Lane Tearoom** is

the BEST Bakeries

Deanston Bakery

always a treat. Then, there's **Seb & Mili** and **Singl-End** – ask for their millionaire's shortbread.

Deanston Bakery is a Southside favourite with best-sellers including cinnamon buns and bagels. The sourdough bread from social enterprise **Freedom Bakery** is part of the menu in some of Scotland's top restaurants. Plus, you'll notice **Twisted Empire Bakes'** distinctive modern take on empire biscuits in many of the city's leading cafes and look out for **Kitty's Doughnuts** on local cake stands.

KAF, part of the weekend tradition in Partick when it was a café, has converted to a local bakery, making things like rye bread and porridge loaves. They've recently introduced their own chocolate bar, the KAFFO, a collaboration with Heist Chocolate. You will also find excellent coffee.

KIRTSY ANDERSON

What would you miss most Glasgow if you moved to another city?

It would have to be the Glasgow humour, there's nothing quite like it.

Where is your favourite place to eat in Glasgow, apart from DVBC?

My favourite places to eat are your classic Glasgow cafes. Unpretentious working-class environments where you always feel at home, nothing beats a coffee and a Mortons roll.

Where would you take your best pal for a pint?

It would have to be Bloc+ on Bath Street. It is still a local institution and a place I will always hold deeply in my heart. Many years I spent in that building with some of the maddest folk you can imagine. Pints and nostalgia and all the patter to match.

What's your favourite park or outdoor space in the city?

Queen's Park, it's on my doorstep, it's an amazing resource for the local community. You cannae beat a bit of breathwork in the bushes. Daytime only of course. I hosted free Sunday sunrise meditation classes post-lockdown there.

There's also loads going on, and it's a hub for inner-city nature and wildlife. For a place that is such a concrete jungle in parts, Glasgow has some epic gems and Queen's Park is one of them.

How did you end up running a Vegan Burger Club?

I had been running Durty Vegan Burger Club as a pop-up for a few years waiting for the time to be right. Glasgow's plant-based scene has dramatically grown over the last few years and sometimes you have to wait patiently for concepts and ideas to break and for people to get what you're trying to do.

My progression into this was a

Champion of the Vegans

Danny McLaren's journey goes from Easterhouse via Bloc+ to setting up Durty Vegan Burger Club with a view of the Finnieston Cran

natural one. When you've worked your arse off for several years in kitchens, you will inevitably want to pursue your own ideas and have your shot at bringing something you can be proud of to the food scene.

You recently had your own show on BBC Scotland, The Scran Van, what was that like?

I always knew I was born for the telly. I absolutely love it. It's something I've been excited about for a long time. I also love people and love my city. I feel I can really push that across on TV, and represent

a true version of Glasgow, we're a city like no other, with more passion and determination than anywhere else I've seen.

Do you have any tips for anyone trying to run a small creative business in Glasgow?

Be prepared to sacrifice your life and learn how to keep getting back up, time and time again. This game is not for the faint-hearted, especially if you have a strong vision and ethos in mind for what you want to create. You must have complete faith in yourself and not care what anyone else thinks, be prepared to risk everything, make losses and failures, and still get back up each day unshaken and still as determined and driven as you were on day one.

🌐 durtyveganburgerclub.com
📍 994 Argyle St, G3 8LU

GLASGOW'S TOP 20
COFFEES

1 Papercup

They started out here introducing specialty coffee and attracting the brunch bunch in 2012. Since then they have built a reputation for a top espressos and meals featuring organic meats and fresh farm eggs. In normal times, expect "positive vibes and uplifting tunes". The kind of relaxed, friendly neighbourhood café that you would like at the end of your street. Order the muffuletta: a New Orleans pressed focaccia with cold and cured meats, peppers, olives and cheese.

♀ 603 Great Western Road, G12 8HX

⊕ papercupcoffee.co.uk

2 Spitfire

Spitfire Espresso sits on one of the great vantage points in the Merchant City, across from the Ramshorn Church and with a view of some of the apartment buildings that triggered the next stage of redevelopment on nearby streets. They are a friendly bunch and serve up an excellent cup of coffee.

♀ 127 Candleriggs, G1 1NP

⊕ spitfireespresso.com

3 East Coffee Company

East Coffee Company opened on Duke Street in January 2018. They have flourished as a compact neighbourhood hub for locals and those who appreciate a strong cup of coffee, pancakes in the morning or a slice of banana and walnut loaf in the afternoon. Currently offering takeaway from their roastery on Hillfoot Street.

♀ 30 Hillfoot Street, G31 2LF

⊕ eastcoffeecompany.com

4 The Steamie

A lively Finniestion spot for a chat and an espresso, which they pull through their La Marzocco Linea Classic. A go-to place for picking up equipment for brewing coffee at home. They offer a clean eating snack menu, hearty soups and homemade bakes.

♀ 1024 Argyle Street, G3 8LX

⊕ thesteamie.co.uk

5 Us Vs Them

A recent arrival in the East End, this coffee bar is also

a creative space for the local community. They change their coffee supplier four times a year. Owner James Aitken says: "We are buying coffee that has not been seen in the area. This is exciting for consumers but also for us". Expect future roasts from Seattle and across Europe.

📍 200 Gallowgate, G1 5DR
🌐 usvthem.coffee

6 Primal Roast

A clean-eating cafe opened by crossfit instructor Iain Walker, a former sous chef at Ubiquitous Chip with over 20 years of experience in fine dining. His brother Ross is head barista. The break-

fast menu includes sweet potato hash browns served with poached eggs, two rashers of smoked bacon, tomato relish and spinach, as well as the popular option of mashed avocado and bacon on rye bread.

📍 278 St Vincent Street, G2 5RL
🌐 primalroast.com

7 Short Long Black

Come for the coffee, stay for the pies, baked fresh each morning. Flavours include ham hock, cheese and potato or vegetarian haggis. Look for lemon meringue tart, cinnamon buns, carrot loaf, and chocolate cookies straight out of the oven for dessert.

📍 501 Victoria Road, G42 8RL
📷 shortlongblackcoffee

8 Grain and Grind

They take a global approach to coffee with blends from Tanzania to Guatemala. Look for local Bungo, Marchtown and Queen's Park roasts. Visit for substantial sandwiches, packed flatbread wraps and Kitty's Donuts. They have three locations in the Southside: Pollokshaws Road, Battlefield Road and Clarkston Road.

📍 50 Battlefield Road, G42 9QF
🌐 grainandgrind.co.uk

Riverhill Cafe

9 Andina Coffee Co.

Maria Varela moved from Colombia to Glasgow in 2017 and set out to work with Fair Trade suppliers to bring quality coffee beans from artisan farms in her home country to this small coffee bar on Duke Street. Look for Three Sisters Bake brownies at the counter.

📍 527 Duke Street, G31 1DL
🌐 andinacoffee.com

10 Salmagundi

Mount Florida cafe serves speciality coffee like Sipi Falls and Guadalupe Zaju, both from Thomsons Coffee, on filter. For lunch, order a kimchi toastie with a side of celeriac and pistachio

soup or maybe cauliflower and cumin fritters with hummus, tzatziki, pomegranate jewels and pickled onions, topped with a perfect poached egg.

📍 1007 Cathcart Road, G42 9XJ
📘 cafesalmagundi

11 Black Pine Coffee Co

A bright, welcoming wee coffee shop. They stock cakes from Wild Flours Bakery and will make you a toastie with bread from Freedom Bakery and cheese from near neighbour IJ Mellis.

📍 518 Great Western Road, G12 8EL
🌐 blackpinecoffee.com

12 Riverhill Cafe

A buzzy cafe near Central Station, their coffee is supplied by Dear Green. Cake, sandwiches, savoury pastries and salads alongside daily specials. Try their breakfast bagels.

📍 24 Gordon Street, G1 3PU
🌐 riverhillcoffee.co.uk

13 Willow Grove Coffee

A dog friendly multi-roaster coffee shop on Sauchiehall Street at Charing Cross. Sit in and takeaway orders, morning pastries and waffles, wraps and soups at lunch. Chocolate brownies baked in-house.

📍 531 Sauchiehall Street, G3 7PQ
📘 willowgrovecoffee

14 Good Coffee Cartel

Your friendly neighbourhood environmentally conscious coffee shop. They've been at the forefront of zero waste packaging since they opened in 2017. You can enjoy tasty cakes from Akara Bakery sitting by the window, pick up

Roasters Dear Green Coffee

JAMIE SIMPSON

It all started with one significant purchase. Lisa Lawson had been in Australia, backpacking around. She found a job and learned how to roast coffee. When she came back to Glasgow, she sold wine and then ran a cafe. She still had a keen interest in the coffee world and often thought about everything she'd learned – where and how the beans are grown, their different flavours and preparations. Then came the moment of truth. Lisa bought a second-hand coffee roaster machine. Nine years later, Dear Green roast coffee in the East End and you will find bags of the stuff in cafes and homes across the city.

Lisa also founded the Glasgow Coffee Festival. Unable to use their usual home at The Briggait, this year the event went into the neighbourhoods with discounts and promotions across local coffee shops. "These guys are really talented and they've been hit hard" she says. "Let's show support to the people behind all of these local businesses which enrich our communities and boost our local economy. Go a walk, have a look at the street art and architecture on your way, visit somewhere new, buy a coffee and find out a little about their story."

📞 0141 552 7774
🌐 *deargreencoffee.com*

© GOOD COFFEE CARTEL

merchandise like caps and mugs or order takeaway coffee, including iced coffees.
📍 12 Cornwall Street, G41 1AQ
🌐 thegoodcoffeecartel.com

15 The Glad Cafe

A Shawlands cafe and music venue serving high quality coffee from Machina Espresso and cakes from Big Bear Bakery, alongside gluten free cakes from Wild Flours Bakery. Vegan and vegetarian small plates and a wide selection of craft beers also available. The home of the Glad Community Choir.
📍 1006A Pollokshaws Road, G41 2HG
🌐 thegladcafe.co.uk

16 Gordon Street Coffee

Gordon Street has been roasting their own coffee in small batches here since May 2014. Their Glasgow Roast, available to buy by the bag is a blend of beans from India, Kenya, Brazil and Guatemala for a well-balanced cup of coffee.

Popular with travellers on the go at Central Station, they'll also organise you a breakfast roll in the morning.
📍 79 Gordon Street, G1 3SQ
🌐 gordonstcoffee.co.uk

17 Dandelion Cafe

Two locals, Mairi Darroch and Suzanne Stevenson, took on an abandoned tennis pavilion and set about restoring it as a 1920s arts and crafts revival cafe. They've succeeded, creating a cosy cafe for brunch, cake and coffee.
📍 Newlands Park Pavilion, 26 Lubnaig Rd, G43 2RY
🌐 cafedandelion.wordpress.com

18 Honey & Salt

Vegetarian cafe serving sourdough toasties, plant-based snacks and baking. Fresh bread daily. Try a tahini swirl and roasted pistachios brownie with a Brazilian flat white or El Salvador black coffee.
📍 25 Carmunnock Road, G44 4TZ
📷 honeyandsaltcaoffeebar

© HONEY & SALT

19 BAM Glasgow

Speciality coffee from guest roasters and homemade cake

© BAM

alongside vintage items, gifts and cards to buy. A coffee shop with a lot of personality.
📍 44 Nithsdale Road, G41 2AN
🌐 bamglasgow.co.uk

20 It All Started Here

They began as a coffee pop-up at Partick Farmer's Market and Bakery47 when they were on Victoria Road before settling down in a small unit on Deanston Road. They work with roasters from all over Europe and serve cakes, sandwiches and light bites Tuesday to Friday with a slightly bigger menu at weekends. They make everything in-house apart from their bread which is baked by Baikhous in Renfrew.
📍 75 Deanston Drive, G41 3AQ
🌐 allstartedhere.wordpress.com

"My parents wanted me to be a lawyer or an accountant. I wanted the hospitality industry."

SEUMAS MACINNES ARRIVED AT CAFE GANDOLFI in 1983 to peel potatoes and chop red cabbage. By 1995, he'd been a kitchen-porter, manager and co-owner until Gandolfi's founder, Iain Mackenzie, decided to step aside and leave him in charge. Seumas' family connections to Barra informed his approach to food and helped create one of the most popular restaurants in the city.

They take their cooking seriously here and offer a relaxed haven for long lunches or fun evenings with friends.

We sat down for a cup of tea one morning and had a chat about the Gandolfi story, Glasgow restaurants and favourite ingredients.

Gandolfi is one of our favourite places in the Merchant City. It has been a fixed point in an area that has undergone a lot of changes. What has it been like looking out from here and seeing those changes?

So often when you are so involved in your business and hands on as I am, you don't really have a chance to look out and notice what others are doing. Of course, it makes sense to lift your head sometimes.

For me, all the competition around me has been good because before when we were the only business here in 1979 into the early 80s, people often thought they wouldn't get a table here because it was so busy but now people try and if not, they'll go to somewhere else.

The café opened in 1979 and I got involved in 1983. Even then people thought we were a step too far towards the East. It's unbelievable now when you think about it [laughs].

So this was on the wild border territory of the city centre?

This was, it was a step too far for some people. They would get a taxi down from Central Station thinking they were being brave.

Now, the Merchant City is going from strength to strength. I see lots of new places opening, sadly some closing. It's much easier to open somewhere than it is to sustain it.

How does someone go from kitchen porter to owner?

It didn't happen overnight, I can assure you. I had studied hotel management and I had got my chef qualifications. I worked in various places but I needed a part-time job. I worked in the kitchen at various levels, then the manager left and I applied for the job and got it. After managing for six years, Iain Mackenzie asked if I would become a junior partner, which of course I said yes to.

Had that been an ambition?

I've always wanted this. My parents wanted me to be a lawyer or an accountant or something. I wanted the hospitality industry.

So that was a great opportunity for you, being invited in?

It was. Then Iain just thought "I've

had enough". This is a kind of hard job. You're constantly fire fighting. If you've got the mentality to cope with it then it is all well and good. Not everyone has. He wanted out and asked if I would buy him out.

I've always been struck by the pictures of the old cafes on the walls here.
That was Iain Mackenzie's work. Remember, we're called Gandolfi after a camera. That was Iain's craft, as a photographer.

It's a rich tradition, the Glasgow café, in all it's different forms. Do you see that as part of what you do here, that you have a strong sense of place?
I think the fact that people use us in such a casual way – and I mean casual in the nicest possible way, it's great seeing a man or a woman come in and they'll have a bowl of soup, maybe a glass of wine, and sit on their own. That's a lovely thing that people feel comfortable to come in on their own. There is a nice informality to this room.

That changes in the evening of course, this room is a bit livelier.
Yes, people use it for lots of different reasons. People come in for a coffee and a chat, tourists, lots of different types of people. They come in to meet pals in the evening. We have a lovely repeat custom base which is really important to me.

Can you tell me about the look of this room, the furniture is very distinctive.
The furniture was the first commission of a man called Tim Stead. His work is seen in the Museum of Modern Art in Glasgow. He's thought of as a very important furniture maker, although he considers himself more of a sculptor.
  The furniture is from 1979 and Iain knew of Tim's work because both of them were at art school.

So we're very privileged to have this furniture. When you think of the restaurants that have not been refurbished in 40 years.

In terms of the ingredients that are the core Gandolfi staples, why did black pudding appear on the menu?
Because I come from a culture that makes its own. My mum would make her black pudding and so would my gran. I brought things that we had at home into the restaurant, like the haggis is from Dingwall and that's the one that my mum would buy. Macleod & Macleod (*macleodandmacleod.co.uk*) are my favourite black pudding maker and that was because my wife's mother uses them. When my brother lived in Stornoway, that's what he used.

I like the idea that ingredients that we do very well in Scotland, like fish and black pudding and haggis, we're learning to do other things to them than just put them in the fryer.
Absolutely, I think we have more

of a pride in our own produce. Haggis, Arbroath smokie, black pudding, our cheeses. And also our raw materials like our game and meat and seafood. We saw the world wanting it and thought, we better start using it. I think all over Scotland, things are much better.

I presume that you'll have customers that have been coming here for a long time, it might be different generations of a family at this stage.
Oh gosh yes. They come as children with their parents, maybe at university on their own or when they start work, then you see them as adults, then they start bringing their own babies. It's wonderful.

Do you have a strong sense of identity as a Glaswegian?
Oh, I'm a Glaswegian. Absolutely. We're so proud of our city. I love that. When people come here as tourists, people want to tell them about their history and want them to have a good experience.

The dining room is a work of art

GLASGOW'S BEST HOTELS

Some of the best places to stay in and around the city, which can also be visited for food and drink or top views.

Afternoon Tea with a View
RADISSON RED

📍 25 Tunnel Street, G3 8HL
📷 radissonredglasgow

The view from the Sky Bar at Radisson RED takes in a sweep of landmarks along the river then the towers of the West End with hills in the far distance. It's worth visiting just to sit there for a while and enjoy the connection with wider Glasgow. Rod Stewart is a fan. There's further reasons to visit since the hotel relaunched their quirky afternoon tea offering, which comes with added gin. Expect a picture perfect and intriguing assembly of tasty morsels. There's familiar elements like a fruit scone with strawberry jam and Chantilly cream or a pork and apple sausage roll but then there's also extravagant touches like mini Southern fried crispy chicken on a hot waffle with barbeque sauce and Asian style

confit duck in plum sauce served in a bao bun. The smoked bacon and sweet maple doughnut and mini red velvet cake provide a sugar rush. Make sure to book a table by the window. The hotel rooms feature specially commissioned artwork by Glasgow comic book artist Frank Quitely.

Destination Dining
CROSSBASKET CASTLE

📍 Stoneymeadow Road, High Blantyre, G72 9UE
🌐 crossbasketcastle.com

Dinner at Crossbasket Castle has a real sense of occasion. The luxury hotel has hosted a series of dinner events in its restaurant this year, with menus designed by Michel Roux Jr. How did the celebrated Roux family of Michelin star chefs come to be involved in a restaurant in an historic landmark tucked away beside the East Kilbride expressway? Crossbasket was bought by husband-and-wife Steve Timoney and Alison Reid-Timoney in 2011. They invested over £9 million in renovating the 17th Century castle as a luxury hotel, including adding a 250-capacity great hall. In 2016 a partnership was announced that would see the dining room serve menus in the style of London's Le Gavroche, with an added

focus on local Scottish produce. It's proven to be a winning formula. Since then, the Roux family have been frequent visitors to this outpost of their culinary empire, leading cookery demonstrations and tastings. The absence of wedding functions at the hotel has created a window of opportunity for more evening dining events. With three course meals like langoustine bisque, roast sirloin of Tweed Valley beef and dark chocolate fondant in luxurious surroundings, a leisurely 20 minutes drive from the city centre, traffic permitting, this is the kind of destination dining event that's not to be missed.

Musical Hotel
IBIS STYLES GLASGOW CENTRE WEST
📍 Douglas House, 116 Waterloo Street, G2 7DN
⌾ ibisstylesglasgow

This particular member of the Ibis Styles hotel collection draws its inspiration from Glasgow's musical heritage. Rooms have names of famous local bands on prints, the stars from the famous Barrowlands sign on headboards and other design cues that give a strong sense of place. The bar area on the ground floor has become a daytime meeting place with plenty of space for distancing. It will soon return to being a buzzy bar and dining area for guests and folk from nearby Financial District offices. It sits at a convenient position for those arriving at Central Station, on their way to the West End for a gig or a night out.

Cocktail Hour
DAKOTA
📍 179 W Regent Street, G2 4DP
🌐 dakotahotels.co.uk/glasgow

Uber-stylish yet retaining a sense of local informality, Dakota's hotel bar is the place

to find creative cocktails and a cosmopolitan atmosphere. They've also a private room for small parties, a more sedate library foom and an outside terrace. An old Works and Pensions building close to Sauchiehall Street was transformed into a modern boutique hotel by Glasgow hotelier Ken McCulloch and his designer wife Amanda.

Hotel Restaurant
HOTEL DU VIN ONE DEVONSHIRE GARDENS
📍 1 Devonshire Gardens, G12 0UX
🌐 hotelduvin.com/glasgow

One of the city's most glamorous addresses, Hotel Du Vin at One Devonshire Gardens is a boutique hotel played out over a series of individually designed rooms across a pretty row of West End townhouses. The dining room is a culinary marker in the city. Their reputation for fine dining has been enhanced since head chef Gary Townsend took over the kitchen in 2017. Visit for elegant seasonal dishes, find a comfy corner of the bar across the corridor afterwards for a large gin or whisky.

Penthouse Apartment
NATIVE GLASGOW
📍 14 St Vincent Place, G1 2EU
⌾ nativegla

There are more extravagantly appointed penthouses in the city, but you can't beat the view and the welcome you will find at Native. Their modern penthouse is the jewel in the crown of this popular hotel. It's one of the best places to wake up in the city centre with views of George Square, City Chambers and across the rooftops. Established in an impressive Edwardian building, formerly home to the Anchor Line Shipping Company's headquarters, this distinctive hotel features 64 apartments, many featuring original 1906 design motifs.

Let's Lounge
KIMPTON BLYTHSWOOD SQUARE HOTEL
📍 11 Blythswood Square, G2 4AD
🌐 kimptonblythswoodsquare.com

When celebrities are in town for inter-

views, musicians are performing at The Hydro or football players arrive to sign for a new team, they often stay here. When a fire alarm went off recently, both Billy Connolly and Ariana Grande found themselves evacuated from suites and deposited on the street. Hugh Jackman has hosted after-show parties in the glamorous hotel restaurant. On the first floor is the lounge, a grand salon where you can enjoy afternoon tea or gather on Harris Tweed chairs for an evening of cocktails and a view over the square.

Budget Stay
MOTEL ONE
📍 78-82 Oswald Street, G1 4PL
🌐 motel-one.com/en

Right beside Central Station, Motel One is part of the next wave of Glasgow hotels. The budget hotel by the German chain

offers no-frills accommodation right beside Central Station. The big, open-plan lobby area and bar are dotted with statement-piece accessories, sofas and armchairs.

Resort Hotel
MAR HALL
📍 Earl of Mar Estate, Bishopton, PA7 5NW
🌐 marhall.com

A 20-minute drive west along the Clyde from the city centre, via the M8, and you find yourself in tranquil seclusion on a 240-acre woodland estate. It's that easy to escape to a spa and golf resort with accommodation in a five-star grand mansion, the former Erskine House, complete with ornamental fountain and gardens. Guests who have stayed in the hotel include Bob Dylan, Kylie Minogue, Liam Gallagher and Katy Perry, although not all on the same night.

Glasgow is making outstanding craft beer, with interesting stories. Meet some of the people driving the rise of local independent brewing.

Words: David Kirkwood

PICTURE THE SCENE: YOU can't leave your house, you can't go to the pub... You find out that a local brewery have just launched a new beer. You order it online and that very afternoon the chilled cans are delivered to your door. It's a beautiful moment. Thank you, Overtone. This team hit the ground running in 2018 after brewer Dan Miller and director Bowei Wang set up in Yoker, on the Western tip of the city.

Miller comes from New Hampshire, and appropriately, their house style is the 'NEIPA' (translation: New England IPA), which has been the dominant trend in craft beer over the last couple of years – beers which are more tropical and juicy, and less bitter than other types of IPA.

Overtone have surfed that wave with aplomb, exporting to ten countries and attracting increasingly enthusiastic reviews for their hazy, vibrant brews. They've maintained a solid on-the-ground presence too: Turning out beers most weeks and getting them into all the main bars in the city. When lockdown happened, Overtone adapted. Fast. "We've always had a canning

A new wave of Craft brewing

line and sold to independent craft shops", points out Head of Sales James Kidd, "but one of the defining moments for us was being able to sell direct to customers. It was the third week of lockdown that we were granted the license, and it meant that we could still make beer, and have a route to market during that period". That was when the guys really found their form, with their 'Lost In Translation' series of beers including 'Weegie', 'Yaldi' and a 10 per cent triple IPA called 'Big Yin'.

🌐 *overtonebrewing.com*

ACID BREWING CARTEL'S operation is somewhat more ad hoc. The collective is in fact one Ciaran Febers, who has taken 'cuckoo brewing' (translation: a brewer makes beer at someone else's brewery because they don't have their own) to exciting levels. His first beer, 'Acid Mango', was brewed at Drygate and was launched as an Italo-Disco club night in the Merchant City.

"I love sour beers, I love Italo, and Pete Sansom from Drygate showed me a few tips early on... so it just made sense!" he says. That's

The Bottle Shop

CHICAGO'S Jehad Hatu introduced us to growlers – a fancy sealable jug that you pour beer into to takeaway – in 2016. Grunting Growler has six taps, backed up by hundreds of cans and bottles.

He is passionate, creating a whole space with his enthusiasm. A year after opening, GG got its tasting licence and that meant customers could hang out and drink in-store. Is it a pub?

"Nah, I'm not doing this to turn the shop into a bar – I want to turn the shop into an experience".

The unit is a perfect example of why local independent businesses should be treasured for the extra level of care and expertise that will make the visit more fun. They run tasting nights, basic introductions to beer styles, through to leftfield evenings matching beers with donuts. He's not concerned by the expanding range of craft beers in the supermarkets these days. "The choice has improved and that's great if you're a beer drinker. But they're getting in new stuff every couple of months – we get 20 new beers a week".

📍 51 Old Dumbarton Rd, G3 8RF ☏ 0141 258 4551
🌐 gruntinggrowler.com

---

the sort of delightful chemistry that makes for a strong grassroots scene in the city.

Acid Brewing's beers are niche, quirky, and hit hard. There was 'A Tribe Called Zest' that he made with fellow Glaswegians, Ride; and there was 'Make Acid Great Again', with Campervan over in Leith. Then came 'Industrial Farmhouse' – in a champagne bottle, using an ancient strain of Norwegian yeast, that he had to source from a Bristolian man living in Budapest. "It is without doubt the craziest beer I've brewed to date" he laughs.

"It was so fruity, and people were shocked when they found out there was no actual fruit added." The flavour was from the embers in the yeast, apparently.
📷 *acid.brewing.cartel*

NEXT YEAR WILL SEE the debut of new contenders Mouthpiece. Their credentials are impressive: the team – Nina Martin, Alex Martin and Lynsey Cameron – are all familiar faces in the Glasgow bar scene, fostering those existing ties with "beer that's fun, beer that people want to drink, beer that bars want to sell". That's Cameron's refreshingly frank take on proceedings.

There's a creative pulse to their operation, with a big interest in street art and graphic design.

She elaborates: "yes, we want folk to enjoy buying our cans because the artwork's cool and the beer is easy drinking, but also because people know who we are and what we're about."

With women taking on the roles of managing director and creative director, Mouthpiece are aware they have an opportunity to redress the balance somewhat in terms of who makes beer and who influences beer tastes in the city.

So their name, and their logo – a snarling mouth – are entirely appropriate. Nina laughs: "we've definitely got something to say.

Mouthpiece enter the craft beer scene. Dennistoun mural by Ciarán Glöbel and Conzo Throb

Our social media account will be very active, talking about issues that matter to us – equality, environment, accessibility – and making sure people from all genders and walks of life find us approachable".

They've an unofficial agreement to smile in photographs.

Mouthpiece are currently securing the right space for a brew kit to introduce their first beer – a 'strawberry kolsch', which will be a Cologne-style lager made with added Scottish strawberries, which Alex and Nina originally brewed for the guests at their wedding.

GLASGOW'S TOP 5
BURGERS

1 El Perro Negro

Dreamed up by Nick Watkins who started out with events that established demand for their Top Dog burger – a rare-breed beef patty topped with slices of rare-breed bacon, then bone marrow and roquefort butter, caramelised onions and black truffle mayo on a toasted brioche bun. It's a thing of beauty. A neat little permanent base opened in Finnieston with backing from The Gannet co-owners and chefs Peter McKenna and Ivan Stein, followed by a neighbourhood burger joint in Woodlands. Organic and free-range beef from Peelham Farm. Nick went to London

and defeated competition from Gordon Ramsay's Bread Street Kitchen and some of the leading restaurants in the country to win the National Burger of the Year title. Their recent special for National Burger Day shows that they like to go big on their burgers: "Double smash, double cheese, double bacon, marrow butter, burnt butter mayo,

pickles and onions".

📍 152 Woodlands Rd, G3 6LF 📞 0141 248 2875
🌐 el-perro-negro.com

2 Bread Meats Bread

Bread Meats Bread's high-impact combinations include the ridiculously indulgent Luther Burger – a double smashed burger with American cheese,

candied bacon, spicy beefy mayo and crispy fried onions inside a grilled glazed ring donut to turn the taste levels up to eleven. It's food to put a smile on your face. They serve up big flavours from Great Western Road and The Fort with a bigger city centre branch replacing their original St Vincent Street headquarters in recent months. The menu includes gluten free and halal options. Order a portion of caramelised sweet potato fries, with maple syrup, cayenne pepper and coconut to accompany your burger. A sensational side.

📍 701 Great Western Rd, G12 8RA 📞 0141 249 9898
🌐 breadmeatsbread.com

3 Dennistoun Bar-B-Que

The food has American sensibilities, but the attitude is pure Glasgow. It's a heady mix. One of the main attractions on Duke Street. Currently serving takeaway. Order at the counter, wait as burgers are seared on a hotplate and loaded up with tasty topping, then take your food home. Gather lots of napkins – this is messy eating – and dig in. Their locally sourced meats are smoked in-house using imported Texas oak. They always have an interesting selection of North American and Mexican sodas to go with your meal.

📍 585 Duke St, G31 1PY 📞 0141 237 7200
📷 dennistounbbq

4 Lebowskis

This hip Finnieston hangout has the best White Russian cocktails in town and a selection of intriguing burgers. They are known for attention-grabbing specials, unveiling The Glasgow Oyster, a meaty double beef burger with melted mature cheddar, topped with a scotch pie and beef dripping gravy. To prove they are living their best burger life they are also known to offer square sausage as a topping. Serving up since 2007, mix things up on your next visit with chicken katsu or slow-smoked pulled pork shoulder burgers. The gutterball, their local version of a White Russian is Buckfast, Kahlúa coffee liqueur and milk.

📍 1008 Argyle Street, G3 8LX 📞 0141 564 7988
lebowskis.co.uk

5 Bar Bloc+

Plenty of folk spend their entire social life bouncing between the subterranean bars of Bath Street. The names of the places change but the crowd seems to stay the same. Bloc+ stands out. Not for everyone proclaims the neon sign on the back wall. Yet the menu caters as easily for vegans or vegetarians as it does for hungover folk in need of comfort food. Their quirky burgers with toppings including haggis, onion gravy, sweet pickles and, occasionally, mashed up crisps, have known restorative powers. Add gentle chat from the staff, a pint of Williams Bros lager and some Irn Bru pulled pork fries and you'll be back on top form.

📍 117 Bath Street, G2 2SZ 📞 0141 574 6066
📷 blocglasgow

Clyde-built Fashion

NSPIRED BY GLASGOW'S INDUS-trious heritage, nascent local fashion brand Finnieston Clothing have introduced a line of clothes inspired by Clyde shipyards of the past. The collection uses Scottish lambswool, weatherproof textiles and organic cotton to create Clyde-built t-shirts and jackets from designs based on vintage photographs. They feature details including replica badges and logos unearthed by local historian Ian Johnston.

Ross Geddes, founder of Finnieston Clothing, first launched the label after being inspired by the local creative community. "I knew it had to be a Scottish brand. Even if people don't get the connection to Glasgow, I've found international customers think Finnieston is a nice sounding name. This year I saw a chance to do something that connected to the city's industrial heritage."

What followed was a deep-dive into the folklore of the shipyards. "Ian is a family friend, he has an attic that's basically a museum, I used to go there once a week, we'd look through these amazing old pictures and I was struck by the collarless jackets I saw and the shipping or yard logos, the fonts

and the stories behind each one.

"It was old writing that I liked and enjoyed. I knew there was something untapped that hadn't

Finniestosn Clothing's Ross Geddes wearing some of the latest collection.

ANDREW JACKSON @CURSETHEGEEYES

been explored before in a clothing line. One of the jackets we've produced is based on workwear I saw in pictures of riveters. The clothes are industrial-inspired but they still feel very current."

Ross explains one of the t-shirts has text lifted from a picture taken at the Fairfield shipyard in 1915. "We took the text from a picture – there's five guys, submarine engineer apprentices and they are standing in front of a board, it's almost like their class picture. We've reproduced the writing and made sure it is true to the history. The same for the John Brown & Co t-shirt".

Ross says the research has really captured his imagination and he is now starting to get involved with local groups devoted to promoting and preserving Glasgow's shipbuilding heritage. The fashion pieces have struck a chord with a new generation: "We've had a lot of young guys getting in touch with us through the website, they are ordering some of the range because their granda worked in one of these yards and the clothes are a way for them to connect to their own family story and I love to hear that."

⊕ *finniestonclothing.com*

SHOP LOCAL

Some of the stories behind Glasgow businesses

Forty Clothing

Custom Builds
CURIOUS DESIGN COMPANY
 thecuriousdesignco

At the start of lockdown, Chris Burke found that his company's bar contracts were on hold and he was facing a period without work. With time on his hands, the creative designer was asked to make a toy kitchen for a friend's daughter. More orders followed and Curious Design Company was formed with ideas for garden chalkboards, climbing frames and play parks for nurseries alongside custom furniture. They hope to continue to work on building projects and develop new products. There's also plans to convert a vintage pickup truck into a coffee bar and a trailer into a Curious Cocktail Bar.

Prints and Fashion
SOCIAL RECLUSE
 48 King Street, G1 5QT
 thetenten.co.uk/artist/social-recluse

Social Recluse create prints and t-shirts to a soundtrack of music, fashion, football and subculture. Founder Robert Chalmers quit his job ten years ago to concentrate on screen-printing and design.

"I started off with ten t-shirts a week, then football fans got into it, then I started doing merchandise for Glasgow bands and it all built up from there."

Inspired by classic styles, he began to put images of trainers together with albums and singles for a collection which have proven popular.

Wearable Art
1 OF 100
 weare1of100.co.uk

This independent brand sends creative fashion items from West Regent Street to the world. Their recent collaboration with author Ian Rankin was a sell out success and the literary and musical inspiration is set to continue. The core idea is printing on demand, limited-edition t-shirts, sweatshirts and tote bags.

"I wanted to do something to be creative and I took a lot of inspiration from limited edition records and the idea that you could make something with a finite number of them available that would last, would be valued and could bring a bit of joy to people" founder Richie Hume says.

Diamonds & Thrills
ROX JEWELLERY
 42-45 Argyll Arcade, G2 8BG
 rox.co.uk

At Rox Jewellery they take advantage of the stylish showroom space they have above the shop - you can relax and enjoy a glass of Champagne and afternoon tea while a range of options are brought to your table, whether it be engagement rings, statement pieces or high end watches.

If you are going to make an important purchase to mark a special moment, you may as well enjoy the experience.

Streetwear
FORTY CLOTHING
11 Royal Exchange Square, G1 3AJ
ortyclothing.com

Harry Miller says streetwear was always his obsession. For him, fashion was tied in with house music and self-expression. "I'm a shop floor guy, I like to find out why people walk through the door, working in retail you'd build up a relationship with folk."

Having a city centre shop is important to him: "We started with a website but in the store, we want to give customers an experience you can only get here."

My Glasgow

CLARE GROGAN
Actress & singer

I HAVE TRAVELED THE WORLD and although I'm biased, I think Glasgow has an amazing amount to offer. The buildings are spectacular, the arts, music and culture scene is incredibly diverse and inclusive. And the curries are the best.

My daughter Elle asked me when she was little if everyone in Glasgow knew each other – I explained that people in Glasgow are the friendliest people I've ever come across. We try to keep that flag waving in London where we live.

My earliest memories here are of growing up in Hill Street and being afraid of the Art School building around the corner. I

remember my great aunt Winnie playing the organ at St Aloysius Church and watching films sitting on my mum's knee at the ABC cinema on Sauchiehall Street. Our neighbours, the Capaldis, gave me and my sisters Margaret and Kathleen chewing gum – which we were not allowed. I also remember my Dad's spag bols. And new shoes from Clarks at the start of every school term.

I have lots of great memories of family life as well as a few painful ones. My Mum and Dad brought me and my two sisters up to respect the people around us and to think big. They really didn't have much, but we never felt like we did without. They taught us to value things.

Good parenting is not easy, I now know first hand but I still think about what their view would be. They really were a bit differ-

ent, which explains quite a lot about who me and my sisters are. I went to Notre Dame, it was just school to me but I met one of my best friends there, Elizanne. We are still occasionally like naughty school girls together.

I had my first cappuccino in the Cafe Gandolfi – still one of my favourite places to meet and eat. I also love the Kelvingrove Gallery – my parents took us when we were little and I go every year. It's particularly amazing if someone is playing the organ.

I love the Centre for Contemporary Arts and I love the Citizens Theatre – where I saw my first naked man!

I can't leave out the No 59 bus...don't

Memories of the Kelvingrove (left and and Centre for Contemporary Arts (right)

know if it's still a thing, but it took me everywhere I needed to go and I had the best laughs at the back of the bus on it.

When I think of Glasgow I think of crossing the Kingston Bridge and looking both ways down the Clyde.

It's still one of my favourite places to shop and I still love running occasionally to all the corners of Bellahouston Park where I used to run when we moved to the Southside. I also of course think of my parents who have now moved on together to heaven. I love Glasgow every which way – it's in every bit of me.

Victorian Chic
STARRY STARRY NIGHT
📍 19 Dowanside Lane, G12 9BZ 📞 0141 337 1837
🌐 starrystarrynightvintage.co.uk

Opened in 1986, this picture perfect shop, located down Dowanside Lane in the west end, is home to treasures from various eras, such as antique clothing that dates back to Victorian and Edwardian times, as well as retro clothing from the 60s-80s. Shoppers can also browse vintage textiles, costume jewellery and handbags.

Tailcoats & Gowns
RETRO CLOTHING
📍 8 Otago Street, G12 8JH 📞 0141 576 0165
🌐 retro-clothes.com

Retro Clothing is one of a few west end vintage shops and stocks a range of clothes for men and women – from tailcoats and evening gowns to Victorian lace and 60s and 70s flares. There's also a range of vintage bedding, jewellery and accessories to complete the retro look.

Levi's to Burberry
THE GLASGOW VINTAGE CO
📍 453 Great Western Rd, G12 8HH 📞 0141 338 6633
🌐 glasgowvintage.com

For anyone that remembers and still misses Watermelon, a cosy vintage destination turned coffee shop on Great Western Road, a trip to the much roomier Glasgow Vintage Co is a must. Established in 2011 by Gavin and Mari O'Brien, previous owners of Watermelon Vintage, this independent shop

Starry Starry Night

Find your favourite era at this selection of local clothes shops

stocks a wide range of retro clothes for men, women and children with names such as Wrangler denim, Burberry, Harris Tweed, Barbour and Levi. Items are from the 50s to the 90s and sourced from all over the UK and Europe.

Classic & Current
MR BEN
📍 Unit 6, Kings Court, G1 5RB 📞 0141 553 1936
📷 mrbenretroclothing

One of the longest established retailers of vintage clothes and accessories, Mr Ben has been on the radar of students and those looking for a bargain or quirky buy since the 90s. An emporium of vintage, shop-

pers can spend hours browsing the range of designer, classic and labelled clothing and accessories, which span some of the most influential and recognisable decades in fashion.

GLASGOW AT HOME

If you are looking for watercolour prints, retro furniture or statement pieces to dress your house, here's how you find them. A guide by *Rosalind Erskind* and *Aline Browers*.

Fabrics

MANDORS

📍 134 Renfrew Street G3 6ST 📞 0141 332 4221
🌐 *mandors.co.uk*

Whether you're making a new shirt or in the market for updated curtains, Mandors is the place to go. A Glasgow institution –

the fabric shop opened in the city centre in 1977 on Scott Street before moving to Fleming House – it is home to everything from dressmaking fabrics to patchwork and quilting fabrics to bridal. You'll also be able to shop hard to find fabrics such as hessian, baize and plastic coated as well as knitting yarns and needles – a crafters haven.

Classic Interiors

CHELSEA MCLAINE

📍 157 Milngavie Road, G61 3DY 📞 0141 942 2833
🌐 *chelseamclaine.co.uk*

Owner Margot Paton founded Chelsea Mclaine in 1992 with a vision to create timeless yet original interiors. Often featured in homes magazines, Chelsea Mclaine also has a shop on Hyndland Street as well as the original showroom in Bearsden. Services include lighting design, kitchen and bathroom design and supply, and soft

furnishings and upholstery. Think plush accessories and striking patterns brought expertly together.

Beautiful Bedlinen

BLUEBELLGRAY

📍 162 Hyndland Road, G12 9HZ 📞 0141 221 0724
🌐 *bluebellgray.com*

Bluebellgray has been bringing ethereal watercolour prints into homes since the business was founded by Fi Douglas in 2009. Originally a range of just six cushions created by Fi, Bluebellgray has gained a cult following and is now stocked worldwide. Small, extremely popular sample sales from the beautiful Park Circus office lead to a dedicated shop, which opened on Hyndland Street in 2018. The range spans curtains, bedlinen, cushions, rugs, lighting and accessories, with a new collection of prints released twice a year.

Quirky Buys
GALLETLY AND TUBBS
📍 439 Great Western Road, G4 9JA 📞 0141 357 1002
🌐 galletlytubbs.com

Just off Kelvinbridge, Galletly and Tubbs have home accessories that range from the eclectic to classic, quirky, contemporary and chic. Owners Ma rk Galletly and James Blair brought together their complementary styles and ideas to offer furniture, lighting, artwork, and fabrics and wallpaper.

Eye-Catching Prints
TIMOROUS BEASTIES
📍 384 Great Western Road, G4 9HT 📞 0141 337 2622
🌐 timorousbeasties.com

Chances are you'll have seen a distinctive Timorous Beastie print in a hotel or high-end restaurant. Best known for their bee, Glasgow toile and thistle print, the design company, which specialises in printed wallpapers and fabrics, was established in 1990

by Alistair McAuley and Paul Simmons, *(above)* who met while studying at the Glasgow School of Art. Located in a small building on Great Western Road, which belies the company's international reach and award-winning status, Timorous Beasties has collaborated with Famous Grouse, Nike, Fortnum & Mason, and Philip Treacy.

Colour
LEILA TALMADGE
🌐 leilatalmadge.co.uk

Interior designer Leila made the move to Glasgow from London bringing her love of bold colours and style with her. Mixing modern and vintage to create functional

and beautiful homes and commercial spaces with a focus on colour, Leila also likes to add a unique aspect to each room – an upcycled piece of furniture or a hand-made lampshade.

Secondhand Chic
SALVATION GLASGOW
📞 07788702317
🌐 salvationglasgow.com

Based in the Southside, Salvation has a selection of curated vintage pieces of furniture, lighting and accessories. The small business aims to preserve and revive worn out and damaged items to showcase the quality workmanship that went into them. Brands include G Plan, Morris of Glasgow and Ercol. Sales are online and their social media is the best place to get updates on the one-off items available to buy.

Nomad Design
NIKI JONES
📍 13 Bank Street, G12 8JQ 📞 0141 556 2462
🌐 niki-jones.co.uk

Founded in 2009 by designer Niki, this boutique company is an ideal way to bring the world into your home. In her products,

Niki combines different cultural references with a love of traditional technique, natural materials and colour – creating a stylish collection of textiles, accessories and rugs. Niki's Isosceles collection is woven in Scotland by a family owned mill that was established in 1797.

Cool Cushions
NIKKI MCWILLIAMS
🌐 nikkimcwilliams.com

The humble Tunnock's teacake and caramel wafer are enshrined in cushion form ready to grace the sofas of fans all over Scotland and beyond thanks to designer Nikki McWilliams. Nikki set up her company in 2009 and creates fab, funky accessories that are inspired by pop art and nostalgia. Her tea break collection also includes Nice biscuits, bourbons and custards creams as well as the famous Tunnock's chocolates.

Antiques
GLASGOW CITY ANTIQUES
📍 121, 127 Lancefield Street, G3 8HZ 📞 0141 248 7914
🌐 glasgowcityantiques.co.uk

If you're after something for your home that has a story, then head to Glasgow City Antiques. Stocking everything from antique and second hand furniture covering styles such as arts and crafts and art deco as well as art nouveau. There are roughly 35 dealers under one roof, and you'll also find vintage, collectables and jewellery for sale. A real Aladdin's cave.

Reclaimed Interiors
GLASGOW ARCHITECTURAL SALVAGE
📍 1 Albion Centre, 1394 South Street G14 0BJ
🌐 glasgowarchitecturalsalvage.co.uk

Glasgow Architectural Salvage is the place to shop for Glasgwegians with period properties. Stocking everything from fittings and fixtures such as door handles to fireplaces, ranges and sanitaryware, this is the place for stepping into the past. Their newly designed website shows off some of the products for sale, but for those looking for something specific, just ask. The team can also help locate items and carry out some restoration work, such as cutting doors to size and stripping back to original wood.

Understated Style

HOOS

📍 715 Great Western Road, G12 8QX
🌐 hoosglasgow.co.uk

This independent homeware and lifestyle destination is a 'blink and you'll miss it' wee shop close to Óran Mòr in the west end.

Stock includes names from Nordic design houses, such as Ferm Living and Muuto for home, as well as kids' toys and jewellery and accessories from local artisans. Hoos also has a range of plants and fresh wildflowers from Dear Green Flower Farm – a community run flower farm that grows wildflowers just up the road in the Botanics.

Luxe Tiles

NOMA LIVING

📍 79 Great Western Road, G4 9AH 📞 0141 332 5072
📷 noma_living

Opened in 2017, Noma Living is a kitchen, bathroom and lifestyle furniture showroom focusing on affordable design. Inside you'll find Miele, Sachsenkuechen and Caesarstone. A full wall of eye-catching tiles from Marrakech Design and Ca'Pietra will draw in those looking for the finishing touches to an interior project. Follow them on Instagram for inspiration and finished work from clients.

Bespoke Design

FLOUNCE

📍 493 Great Western Road, G12 8HL 📞 0141 339 1011
🌐 flounce.uk.com

The team at Flounce can offer whatever level of design advice customers need, including bespoke soft furnishings and curtains. They stock brands such as Romo, Zoffany, Casamance, Harlequin and Designers Guild. Their interior design service includes initial design concept meetings and ideas to complete project management.

Vintage Rugs

HOW BIZARRE RUGS

🌐 howbizarrerugs.com

This vintage, handwoven rug emporium is ideal for those looking for something not easily found down the local Ikea. Set up in 2017 by, in their words, "a Scottish lass (Jess) with Persian roots, and a big love for

bold colours, crazy patterns and cosy home furnishings" How Bizarre calls on the memories of Perisan rugs in Jess's family home, and offers buyers the chance to take home an accessory with a story.

Flounce

Found

Upcycled Furniture
FOUND

📍 583 Dumbarton Road, G11 6HY
🌐 foundglasgow.co.uk

Since 2015, Found has been the place to go for design led furniture, upcycled vintage pieces and interesting lighting. You'll also find Newgate clocks, Stolen Form ceramics and, more recently, an impressive selection of stationary. Depending on when you read this, they are preparing to move or have moved to a bigger space further along Dumbarton Road. The shop has grown into a much loved part of the Partick streetscape.

Seaside Vibes
TIME AND TIDE

📍 6 St George's Place, G20 7PW,
also 398 Byres Road, G12 8AR 📞 0141 357 4548
🌐 timeandtidestores.co.uk

Established in 2009 in North Berwick, Time and Tide has expanded to open shops in Edinburgh and Glasgow, on Byres Road and St George's Place in 2013 and 2017 respectively. Stocking bold furniture with a focus on natural material along with chic accessories such as mirrors, clocks and abstract art. Each shop is catered to the local clientele, with Glasgow's stores sporting eye-catching and edgy pieces such as oversized mirrors and dramatic chandeliers.

Kitchenware
AUME

📍 707 Pollokshaws Road, G41 2AA
🌐 aume.co.uk

Aume is a stylish neighbourhood shop for plates, bowls, mugs, glasses and all the rest. You can also pick up rugs, cushions and artwork for your home. Browse through distinctive vases, quirky pots and a vast selection of kitchenware.

Best for Scottish gifts
GIE IT LALDY

📍 199 Crow Rd, G11 7PD
🌐 gieitlaldy.com

In their own words Gie it Laldy celebrates all that is pure dead brilliant about Scots language and culture. Selling a range of cards, gifts, mugs, coasters and pet paraphernalia, Gie it Laldy's early designers were inspired by founder Lisa's much missed gran and have evolved thanks to ongoing dialogue with customers. Celebrating the Scots language, the products are designed, printed and produced in their studio in the west end,

More Local Gifts
BRAW WEE EMPORIUM

🌐 braw-wee-emporium.com

Another great Scottish gift shop, Braw Wee Emporium is the brainchild of Jennifer McGlone who started the business herself, and developed it into a team effort. With a focus on supporting creative endeavours from local craftspeople, Braw Wee Emporium is a one stop shop for cards, crafts and stationery, clothes and bath and body products. The team also run a range of craft workshops, including making gin lamps or cosy blankets – sign up to get in touch with your inner crafty self.

Doorstep Photographer
CARO WEISS

📷 caroweissphoto

An accomplished and established wedding photographer, Caro Weiss spent lockdown taking pictures of Glasgow families and local folk on their doorsteps. The home portraits allowed her to continue her business in the absence of event bookings. Some

CARO WEISS

couples who had to cancel their wedding day got dressed up to have their picture taken in their garden or outside their close. While Caro has returned to her more regular work, if you are looking for an interesting portrait at home, she's the photographer for you.

Sculptures & Props
SORENZO STUDIOS

📍 100 Borron Street, G4 9XG

🌐 *sorenzostudios.com*

They make sculptures, props and prototypes. Started by Thom Wall in 2012 and now a collective capable of making all kinds of different things, from a space helmet to a life-size dinosaur to customised replicas. They also have a molding and casting service. Chat to them if you have some item ideas you'd like translated into real life.

Interior Art
CRISTINA BOYLE

🌐 *christinastudio.co.uk*

Christina Boyle set up her own business offering interior design services, creating mood boards for projects, sourcing inte-

rior finishes and accessories, tackling floor plans. She also creates her own series of paintings which are proving popular as bespoke statement pieces.

Flower Arranging
LITTLE BOTANICA

🌐 *littlebotanica.com*

Gemma Burniston's floral design studio based in Glasgow is mostly devoted to creating flower crowns, seasonal wreaths, hand tied gift bouquets and vase arrangement for events and weddings. You can also

CoLab

sign up for workshops where you can learn some new skills and create your own flower display.

Lifestyle Store
COLAB

📍 11-13 Dowanhill Street, G11 5QS 📞 0141 570 1766

🌐 *colabstore.co.uk*

Created by Peter Mulvenny and Karen Haas as a design-led hub in Partick. The CoLab space takes inspiration from around the world, showcasing stylish products in its retail store. There's also an in-house coffee shop to ponder your next interiors purchase and an event space that's often used by local creatives.

Mid-Century Style
I AM NOMAD

📍 490 Great Western Rd, G12 8EW 📞 0141 337 2791

🌐 *iamnomad.co.uk*

What started as a curated collection of pieces, shown on Instagram in founder Claire Johnston's house, has grown into a shop on Great Western Road. Initially shoppers could head to former buyer and retailer Claire's home for pop-up sales of the accessories and some furniture seen online. These proved so popular that the retail space opened in 2018. Filled with an eclectic mix

of mid century and Danish furniture and modern accessories, there's also a personal shopping, styling and interior styling service available to book to guarantee an insta-worthy home.

Furniture Achive
VINTAGE RETRO

📍 569 South Street, G14 0QX 📞 07803 235 651

🌐 *vintageandretrofurniture.com*

An ever-changing stock of pieces from the 1950s, '60s and '70s with original artwork, chairs, coffee tables, storage and display cabinets. You will find vintage pieces to add a distinctive style to your lounge or dining room, including delightfully retro McIntosh of Kirkaldy furniture. If you are looking for a specific piece to complete the look of your home, they have contacts across the country and can help you find what you are looking for.

My Glasgow

LYNN FERGUSON
Writer & actress

WHEN IN ROME, IT'S good to know not to order off the menu in tourist traps because you'll get scammed. In LA, it's good to know how to drive because the public transport system is really limited. But in Glasgow it's good to have a sense of humour, because everyone you meet could be up for a joke or just generally taking the piss.

My first thought of Glasgow is the bus station – oh the glamour – because that was where I got the bus to and from Cumbernauld. There's a great song by Aztec Camera called *Killermont Street* – takes me there every time.

Sometimes my Mum and I would come to Glasgow on a Saturday. We'd walk down to Goldbergs *(below)* which was bright and full of smiling women with thick orange makeup selling perfume I

couldn't imagine ever being able to afford and weird animatronic animals in the shop windows at Christmas time. Whenever I first read *The Lion, The Witch and The Wardrobe*, I figured Narnia must be something like Goldbergs.

Killermont Street was where I first understood the possibilities of travel as a kid. It blew my mind that they had an actual bus to London. Later

on in life I did get on that bus a couple of times. It was not quite as glamorous as I had thought. It was also at Buchanan Street Bus Station that the smell of bacon sandwiches converted me from vegetarian in my twenties

The Royal Infirmary is where I'd visit my Nana Ingy – who always seemed to be in there for her arthritis. I remember thinking the building was both impressive and scary. I still do. I always figured if you were ill you might want to go somewhere a bit more cosy – somewhere less likely to have ghosts, or Miss Haversham running about in a wedding dress setting fire to things.

One time visiting my Nana – I must have been six or seven because I was wearing green and yellow tea bars and white socks – I was standing on my tiptoes to lean over the big metal radiators in the

ward to look out the huge windows. I was horrified by what I saw. My mum told me it was a Necropolis, but it looked like a straight up graveyard to me. I thought it was pretty ignorant to build a graveyard right outside a hospital when, by the very nature of having to be there, most people were trying not to think about death to start with. It is an amazing building though. Every hospital I've seen since has failed to match its spectacle.

My first flat was in Gladstone Street, St George's Cross. At the time, I was studying at the (then) RSAMD in the now Nelson Mandela Place – so named during the time of apartheid because that's where the South African consulate used to be and in typical Glasgow style, anyone writing to them would also have to write Nelson Mandela Place on the envelope.

I used to love the walk to college, down St George's Road, smirking at the bridge to nowhere at Charing Cross

RICH MARCHEW

(which I note has now been remodeled into an office building) and head down Sauchiehall Street, past Nico's and the alleyway to Maestros and various other scenes of 'personal development" during the 80s – each of which shall remain trapped in the vaults of time.

In the end I had to start getting the subway, because there was a jeweller on Sauchiehall Street doing a deal on ear piercing. I have never been one to resist a bargain, so I was getting a little overburdened in the earring department.

My most recent trips to Glasgow have been for work. Morag Fullarton and April Chamberlaine were lovely enough to put on a couple of my plays at *A Play, a Pie and a Pint* at Óran Mòr. Because it had all started up after I'd left Glasgow, I'd never been there before. I was amazed at how brilliant it was – and yet not amazed at the same time.

Glasgow has always punched well above its weight in terms of theatre, variety, art and music. Glaswegians though don't like to be seen as "up themselves" or "cocky b****ds", which is why Glasgow hasn't been given half the credit it deserves in terms of creative arts. The stuff I learned from Clare MacAulay at the comedy Club in Blackfriars, has served my whole career.

My California grown kids love 'the villagey' feel of Glasgow. They can't understand how me and their dad could have lived there at the same time and yet never met each other. They're so used to everything being a car journey apart, that they are certain that everybody in Glasgow personally knows everybody else. This is further reinforced by the fact that people in Glasgow are willing to openly have conversations with complete strangers, and that when we visited Glasgow a few years ago, they bumped into their cousin Lindsay, Aunty Clare, and family

Ubiquitous Chip

friends Janey and Ashley all driving about in a vintage bus. They figured this was what happened to people in Glasgow all the time. Now I think about it, they're not that wrong.

There are so many places I love in Glasgow. Lunch at Gandolfi. Pottering around the Peoples' Palace or the Botanics. Quick note about the People's Palace: It is virtually impossible to explain the significance of The Big Yin's banana boots to Californian kids, without them thinking you have completely lost the plot.

As darkness falls, pottering around Ashton Lane, stopping off for some posh nosh at Ubiquitous Chip. Then tottering along Great

Blackfriars bar and kitchen

Western Road in the moonlight, marvelling that what you see in front of you is not a film set. Then on towards St Georges Cross, past Cowcaddens – where the Laird used to waggle his wallies – and on towards the bus station where it all began.

Five hundred miles away, and yet the word Glasgow still brings to mind technicolour pictures, music and theatre and drinking and family and bus queues and the wee orange Subway that goes round and round. Christmas shopping when it's cold and dark and rain that doesn't feel like rain, more a kind of mist but it gets you soaked anyway.

Navigating the peril of short people holding umbrellas – one wrong move at the Boots' corner and they could have your blinking eye out. The smell of salt and vinegar from a great chippy. The sound of a smiling woman shouting "Hiiiiyaaah" and of laughter of those now gone.

My eldest son is in his last year at school. I asked him where he wanted to go and study. I told him he could go anywhere in the world. "Easy," he said. "Glasgow". ■

Dear Green Place

The view from Queen's Park. 13.5 per cent of the total area of Glasgow is accessible green space – including 340 play areas, 55 bowling greens and 1,000 hectares of woodland.

ALCHEMILLA
BRIAN MAULE AT CHARDON D'OR
THE BUTCHERSHOP
CAFE GANDOLFI
CAKE BAR
THE DHABBA
EL PERRO NEGRO
GAMBA
THE GANNET
GARY MCLEAN
GLASCHU
THE HUG & PINT
JULIE'S KOPITIAM
ONE DEVONSHIRE GARDENS
PLATFORM
PORTER & RYE
RED ONION
SUGO
SWADISH
UBIQUITOUS CHIP

A GLASGOW COOKBOOK

Recipes from some of the best places that we have written about over the last five years at Glasgowist.com.

Enjoy this snapshot of the local food scene right now and try these dishes at home.

CEVICHE

Fresh white fish, such as sea bream

Peach (summer) or blackberries (autumn/winter)

For the dressing

Lime juice

Elderflower vinegar

Sugar

Salt

"Ceviche is one of those dishes that is unlikely to become a Scottish home-staple, but it's hands down one of our most popular dishes in Alchemilla. It really deserves to be brought to the attention of fish lovers who are willing to give it a go at home.

"Ceviche originated by the Moche civilization in Peru some 2,000 years ago, and then eventually spread into Mexico and Central America. Traditional ceviche, at its most basic, is raw fish marinated in citrus juice and spices; the acid in the juice denatures the proteins in the meat in much the same way as cooking would. The flesh becomes opaque, the texture becomes firmer, yet the flavours remain beautifully fresh: the perfect zingy dish for a light lunch or dinner.

"Here at Alchemilla, we update this dish regularly – adding seasonal elements, such as fruit or herbs. The key to great ceviche is using super fresh fish, so visit your local fishmonger and ask for the best white fish on offer and then give this recipe a try. Serve with a crisp white wine, such as a Pet Nat, to impress your guests." *Head chef, Rory Weymes*

Mix together the lime juice, the vinegar, sugar and salt.

Slice the fish thinly and place into the dressing for 30 seconds .

Plate up the fish and place a piece of the fresh peach or blackberry on the top of each slice.

Drizzle the remainder of the dressing over the top and around the plate.

MICHAEL HUNTER

Alchemilla
1126 Argyle St, G3 8TD
🌐 thisisalchemilla.com
📷 alchemillaglasgow

SLOW COOKED PORK CHEEK
WITH TIGER PRAWN, HONEY GLAZED FIG & BUTTERNUT SQUASH PUREE

Serves 4

For the pork cheeks
4 pork cheeks
1 white onion, diced
2 medium carrots, diced
1 leek sliced
1 whole garlic, crushed
2 rosemary sprigs
4 thyme sprigs
330ml cider
200ml beef stock
Salt and pepper

For the butternut squash
300g butternut squash chopped
50ml double cream
50g butter
1 tsp sherry vinegar

For the tiger Prawns
4 Deveined peeled tiger prawn tails

For the fig
1 Whole fig
1 tbsp Honey

To garnish
Pork crackling
Pea shoots

The Butchershop Bar & Grill
1055 Sauchiehall St, G3 7UD
🌐 butchershopglasgow.com
f butchershopglasgow

Pork cheeks
Season pork cheeks with salt and pepper and seal off in a hot frying pan with olive oil

Place pork cheeks in an oven dish.

Pour beef stock over pork cheeks adding diced white onion, diced carrots, leek, garlic, rosemary, thyme and cider.

Ensure cheeks are covered (top up with water if necessary) cover with tinfoil and bake in oven at 180°C for 2½ hours until meat is soft and tender.

Remove cheeks from beef stock and put to side.

Strain beef stock into a frying pan and reduce to a thick and glossy consistency.

Butternut squash
Boil the squash until soft, strain and place on a tray to dry for 30 mins, to reduce residual moisture).

Heat and reduce double cream and butter in a hot pan.

Place boiled butternut squash, cream and butter reduction into a blender and blitz for a smooth silky texture. Add sherry vinegar and season to taste

Tiger prawns
Pan fry the prawns with butter and seasoning until cooked to preference

Honey glazed fig
Quarter the fig and pan fry with honey for approx. 30 seconds until each piece is warm and slightly soft

To serve
Place 2 tablespoons of butternut squash puree in the centre of the plate. Position pork cheek on top of puree. Drizzle the beef stock reduction over your pork. Place prawn and honey glazed fig to side of pork cheek. Garnish with pork crackling and pea shoots.

MUSHROOM
& CASHEW CURRY

200g unsalted cashew nuts

300g button mushrooms

4 dried shiitake mushrooms

200ml vegetable oil

150g frozen peas

a small handful coriander leaves, chopped

1 medium brown onion, peeled & roughly chopped)

2 green chillies, stalks removed

6 cloves of garlic, peeled

1 thumb sized of ginger, peeled

1 tbsp of palm sugar or brown sugar

1 tsp ground coriander

1 tsp ground turmeric

1 tsp ground cumin

pinch of ground cardamom

pinch of ground fenugreek

1 tbsp of salt

5 fresh curry leaves (frozen is OK, but avoid dried)

1 tablespoon sambal oelek

juice of 1 lime

Cashew nuts blitzed with water and oil into a smooth 'butter' are the key to the richness of this dish, which can stand up to any curry rich with ghee, cream, or animal fat. The comforting creaminess of the cashew butter is countered by sharp and fiery sambal oelek, and balanced with the freshness of peas and coriander.

Inspired by classic Indo-British cuisine, this curry has widespread appeal and is one of our most enduring and popular dishes, appearing frequently on our rotating menu.

In a bowl, cover the dried shiitake in 200ml of hot water and leave to soak for one hour. Meanwhile, in a food processor or a large pestle and mortar, blitz the onion, garlic, chillies and ginger, adding a little of the vegetable oil to achieve a thick paste consistency.

Heat half the oil in a tall saucepan. When the oil is hot but not smoking, add the paste and cook, stirring often, for 30 minutes until it softens and starts to colour.

In a separate frying pan or wok, heat 50ml of vegetable oil and fry the button mushrooms in two batches, until well coloured all over. It helps to keep the mushrooms a similar size, so cut any larger ones in half, keeping the smaller ones whole. Set cooked mushrooms aside.

When the mushrooms are cooked, using the same pan cook half of the cashews over a medium heat until brown, being careful not to burn them.

In a food processor, blitz the remaining untoasted cashews with 100ml of water and 50ml of vegetable oil into a smooth, white butter and set aside.

Add the spices, sugar and salt to the onion/garlic paste and cook for another 20 minutes, adding a bit more oil if it seems dry.

Remove the shiitake from the soaking water and reserve the liquid. Remove the stalks with a sharp knife and discard, then roughly chop the caps and add these to the cooking paste.

Add the mushroom water, cashew butter and sambal oelek to the cooking paste and stir.

Allow the curry to simmer for half an hour on a low heat (or continue to simmer for a few hours which will only result in deeper flavour) then remove from the heat and stir in the peas, coriander and lime juice.

Check seasoning and serve with rice or flatbread.

Top tip
The easiest and most economical way of peeling ginger is with an ordinary dessert spoon (the really lightweight cheap ones are the best). Rub the thin edge of the spoon over the ginger to remove the skin without losing any flesh.

The Hug & Pint
171 Gt Western Rd, G4 9AW
🌐 thehugandpint.com
📷 thehugandpint

CUMIN GARLIC ROAST LAMB

1kg lamb shoulder, boned & rolled

5 red onions, sliced

9 garlic cloves, crushed

15 black olives, chopped

2 tbsp ground cumin

½ tbsp ground cinnamon

½ tsp fenugreek seeds

½ tsp ground all spice

½ grated fresh nutmeg

30ml pomegranate molasses

Salt and pepper

Olive oil

Lamb or chicken stock to cover

For the flatbread

385g self raising flour

385g yoghurt

1tsp baking powder

1g fresh yeast

Pinch of salt

Small handful of caraway seeds

Lamb

Preheat oven to 160°C.

Cut the onions into thin wedges and place in a roasting tray along with the pomegranate molasses, garlic cloves and olives.

Rub the lamb with the spice mix, season well with salt and pepper and drizzle with olive oil.

Pour the hot stock into the base of the tray and cover with foil. Place the tray in the oven for 2.5 to 3.5 hours, then take the tray out of the oven and check the lamb, it should feel tender.

Reserve the cooking liquor, reduce and blend to make your sauce, add this to the lamb and shred the meat.

Flatbread

In a bowl sift flour and baking powder together and rub in the fresh yeast.

Add yoghurt, salt and caraway seeds to flour mix until incorporated. Turn dough onto a work surface and knead for 3 minutes. Place dough back into the bowl, cover and rest for 30 mins. On a floured work surface divide the dough into 6 equal portions, roll each piece out into a circle approximately 3mm thick.

Cook on hot griddle for around a minute and a half, flip and cook for 1 to 2 minutes. Serve with pink pickles, fresh coriander and mint yoghurt.

Platform
253 Argyle St, G2 8DL
🌐 platformgla.co.uk
📷 platform_gla

POLPETTE AL SUGO

Serves 4

For the polpette

250g of beef mince
250g of pork mince
2 eggs
40g of breadcrumbs
1 or 2 leaves of parsley, finely chopped
½ garlic clove, finely chopped
salt

For the sugo

3 tbsp of olive oil
400ml of tomato passata
½ onion, finely chopped
salt
basil leaves, to decorate

Put the meat in a large bowl and mix with your hands.

Add the eggs, the chopped parsley and the chopped garlic, add the breadcrumbs and keep mixing until you obtain a big compact meatball.

Cover the bowl with cling film and let it rest for at least two hours in the fridge for more tender meat.

Now, make some little meatballs from the mixture with a touch of olive oil in your hands. Your polpette are ready to be cooked.

Heat 3 tbsp of extra virgin olive oil in a large pan and place your polpette in it and start cooking them, first on one side and after 2 or 3 minutes, on the other side, using a wooden spoon to turn.

Add the onions and cook them until softened and golden.

Now it is the time for the tomato sauce: pour in and let it cook for 15-20 minutes. Add a pinch of salt and a teaspoon of sugar.

Enjoy with some warm bread.

Accento Cafe
6 Claremont St, G3 7HA
🌐 accentocafe.co.uk
📷 accentocafe

BANG BANG
SALAD

2 skinless chicken breasts
1 tbsp fresh ginger, chopped
2 clove garlic, bashed
½ whole star anise, or a pinch of
    five-spice powder
2 spring onions
½ tbsp peppercorns
1 litre water, or enough to cover
100ml dark soy
30ml shaoxing

For the salad
½ carrot, peeled and shredded/
    julienned into 2cm strips
¼ cucumber, seeded and sliced
½ red pepper fine sliced
2-inch piece daikon radish
1 handful beansprouts
Sesame seeds, lightly toasted
Small handful each of mint and
    coriander leaves
2-3 baby gem leaves

For the dressing
Juice of 1 lime
4 tbsp sweet chilli sauce

For the peanut sauce
150g smooth peanut butter
4 tsp sweet chilli sauce
80ml coconut milk
Zest and juice of 1 lime

Place chicken breasts in a pot that holds them snugly in a single layer.

Add all other ingredients and enough cold water to cover the chicken by 2-3cm.

Bring just to a simmer then cover and simmer for 3 minute. Remove from heat and leave to cool for about 1½ hours.

When ready to use, strain poaching liquid and reserve for later use as stock. Shred the flesh into chunky pieces or slice as preferred.

Empty peanut butter into a bowl, whisk in the chilli sauce, coconut milk and lime zest and juice.

Combine salad dressing ingredients, arrange baby gem leaves on plate, combine all salad ingredients in bowl, dress with salad dressing and mix gently but thoroughly, divide salad between plates, top with chicken, top with peanut sauce.

Red Onion
257 W Campbell St, G2 4TT
🌐 red-onion.co.uk
📷 redonion257

STICKY TAMARIND PRAWNS

Serves 2

16 large raw prawns, deveined, with shell on

1½ tbsp tamarind concentrate

2 tbsp oil

1 stalk lemongrass, finely sliced

2 tbsp dark soy sauce

2 tsp light soy sauce

2½ tbsp palm sugar or brown sugar

dash of salt to taste

Lime juice to taste

Toasted desiccated coconut

100ml water

In a bowl, marinate prawns with the tamarind concentrate, sugar and a pinch of salt (mix everything together and coat well, allow to sit in the fridge in a bowl for at least 30 minutes)

Heat up oil in a wok till it's hot, add in prawns and lemongrass.

Add dark soy sauce, light soy sauce, water and the rest of the marinade immediately.

On medium heat, fry the prawns until the

flesh turns pink and white. When the prawns are almost ready, turn the heat on high and fry for another 2 minutes to get the shells slightly charred and the sauce is a little caramelised.

Add lime juice and salt to taste (and sugar if necessary, depending on how strong the tamarind concentrate you're using is).

Sprinkle toasted coconut on top and serve piping hot.

Julie's Kopitiam
1109 Pollokshaws Rd, G41 3YG
🌐 julieskopitiam.com
📷 julieskopitiam

COLIN MEARNS

GIGHA HALIBUT

WITH CELERIAC, CHARRED HISPI CABBBAGE, POMMES BEARNAISE & PORT REDUCTION

Serves 4

For the port reduction

250ml port
250ml red wine
50g caster sugar
25g red currant jelly
2 cloves of garlic, crushed
10 sprigs of thyme
1 sprig of rosemary

For the chicken butter sauce

1kg chicken carcass/wings
4 cloves of garlic, crushed
10 sprigs of thyme

50ml double cream
100g unsalted cold diced butter
Caster sugar
Lemon juice

For the hispi cabbage

1 hispi (sweetheart) cabbage
Reserved chicken fat
50g unsalted butter, diced
4 cloves of garlic, crushed
5 sprigs of thyme, leaves picked
2g Blackthorn sea salt flakes

For the pommes bearnaise

4 large rooster potatoes
100g unsalted butter
2 cloves of garlic, crushed
4 sprigs of thyme
1 sprig of rosemary
4g Blackthorne sea salt flakes

For the celeriac puree

200g celeriac, peeled and diced 1-1.5cm
50g unsalted butter, diced
1g Blackthorne sea salt flakes
100ml double cream

For the halibut

4 x 150-160g portions of Gigha halibut (hake is a cheaper and equally tasty alternative)
15ml vegetable oil
2g Blackthorne sea salt flakes
100g unsalted butter
10ml lemon juice
100g samphire grass
1 tbsp Lilliput capers, drained but not rinsed
2g flat leaf parsley, chopped

NAOMI VANCE PHOTOGRAPHY

For the port reduction

Place all the ingredients in a pot, bring to the boil. Simmer and reduce to a syrup, then pass through a fine mesh sieve.

For the chicken butter sauce

Place chicken carcasses in a roasting tray and roast at 180°C until golden. Drain and reserve fat, place carcasses, garlic and thyme in a saucepan, deglaze roasting tray with water, add to the saucepan then add enough cold water to cover the roasted chicken carcasses.

Bring to the boil and then simmer for a minimum of 4 hours.

After that time, strain through a fine mesh into another saucepan and leave for half an hour for the fat to settle on top, then skim it off with a ladle and reduce to a sauce consistency (roughly 200ml) it should taste like the most intense roast chicken.

Add the double cream, bring to the boil, remove from the heat and whisk in the diced butter to emulsify. Adjust seasoning with sugar and lemon juice.

For the hispi cabbage

Heat a griddle pan, quarter the cabbage, and coat the flat sides in the reserved chicken fat, seasoning with the sea salt. Place on the griddle flat side down to caramelise.

Once golden-brown, turn to caramelise the other flat side. Remove the cabbage to a roasting tray, top with the garlic, thyme and butter and roast in a preheated oven at 160°C for 8-10 minutes – the cabbage should still have a slight firmness.

For the pommes bearnaise

Peel the potatoes and dice into 2cm cubes, you should get six from each potato, rinse in cold water, transfer to a pot and cover with cold water, season with 2g of the salt and bring the water to the boil, then down to simmer. The potatoes are ready when they are soft but not falling apart.

Remove the potatoes from the water using a slotted spoon, place on a cooling rack, then

Glaschu
32 Royal Exchange Sq, G1 3AB
🌐 glaschurestaurant.co.uk
📷 glaschu_restaurant

place in the fridge for a minimum of 4 hours to cool and allow a skin to form on the outside.

Heat a fryer to 120°C and fry the potatoes until they start to form a nice crust, then transfer to a paper towel-covered tray and again refrigerate for a minimum of 4 hours. Heat a fryer to 180°C and fry the potatoes until golden brown. Heat the butter, garlic, thyme and rosemary in a frying pan until the butter is foaming, add the fried potatoes and season with the remaining sea salt and drain.

For the celeriac puree

Place butter in a pan and melt over a low heat, once melted add diced celeriac and salt, place a lid on the pan and continue to cook on a low heat, moving every few minutes until celeriac is soft.

Once soft add cream, bring to the boil then transfer to a blender and puree. Check the seasoning, as it may require a pinch more salt.

For the halibut

Heat the oil in a non-stick frying pan on a medium heat.

Season the skin side of the fish with half the salt, and place in the pan, then season the flesh side, cook for 1-2 minutes until the edges of the fish start to turn a nice golden brown, then add the butter.

Once the butter is starting to foam, turn the heat down and start basting the fish with the butter for a minute or two, touch the flesh of the fish and it should have started to firm up.

Gently turn each portion over, and using a temperature probe, check the core temperature of each portion, you are looking for a minimum of 75°. Once this is reached, remove the fish from the pan onto a cooling rack, reserve the pan with the butter and fish juices.

Add the lemon juice, samphire, capers and parsley to the pan and return to the heat for 30 seconds and toss to combine then tip into a bowl for garnishing the fish.

GARY MACLEAN

CARROT CAKE

4 eggs
300ml vegetable oil
200g caster sugar
200g light soft brown sugar
2 teaspoons vanilla extract
250g plain flour
2 tsp bicarbonate of soda
2 tsp baking powder
½ teaspoon salt
2 tsp ground cinnamon
350g grated carrots
125g walnuts, chopped

For the icing and filling
125g unsalted butter, softened
200g tub cream cheese,
  softened
125g icing sugar
1 tsp vanilla extract
125g walnuts, chopped

Gary Maclean is Scotland's National Chef, MasterChef the Professionals winner, and Senior Lecturer at City of Glasgow College.

"I don't know who first created carrot cake, but the addition of such a humble vegetable to a cake was an act of genius. This is a perfect recipe for kids to get involved as well."

Preheat the oven to 175°C

Grease and flour two 20cm baking tins.

In a large bowl, beat together eggs, oil, caster sugar and 2 teaspoons vanilla.

Mix in flour, bicarbonate of soda, baking powder, salt and cinnamon.

Stir in carrots and fold in walnuts.

Pour into the prepared tin.

Bake in the preheated oven for 40 to 50 minutes, or until a skewer inserted into the centre of the cake comes out clean.

Let cool in the pan for 10 minutes, then turn out onto a wire rack and let it cool completely.

To make topping and the filling combine butter, cream cheese, icing sugar and 1 teaspoon vanilla.

Beat until the mixture is smooth and creamy.

Spread over the top of cake once it has cooled.

Top with chopped nuts if you wish.

garymacchef.com
gmacchef

NAOMI VANCE

DOUBLE
SMASH BURGER & BACON

160 grams of aged beef mince, course cut, 30% fat.

Burger cheese

Cider vinegar

Raw onion

Large dill pickles

Proper streaky bacon

Mayonnaise (Hellman's)

Good quality butter (unsalted)

Good quality burger buns

"First things first for a good burger you need good beef. I'd recommend a mix with about 30% fat ratio that has a mix of aged beef in it.

"We use large planchas/griddles in the kitchen, but at home you can use a large heavy based pan to cook the burgers." *Nick Watkins*

Burnt Butter Mayo
Place around 100g of butter into a pan and heat until it starts to brown and gives off a nutty aroma. Add straight to 300g mayonnaise and stir vigorously to mix.

Pickle & Onion Garnish
Finely dice onions and pickles to very small cubes (50/50 mix).

Add some of the pickle brine and cider vinegar to taste. It should be sharp, but once the other ingredients are assembled it will cut through richness of beef and mayo.

Burgers
Heat the pan till it's smoking hot and add a wee splash of oil.

Add streaky bacon – you want the bacon to render down and get super crispy. Turn the bacon frequently to ensure it doesn't burn. It shouldn't take any longer than two minutes. Once cooked remove from the pan and put to the side for assembly.

Toast the buns with the remaining bacon fat if you're feeling a bit naughty. For the beef pattys, divide the 160g of beef into two 80g balls. Place the balls in the hot pan leaving a bit of distance between them.

With a large spatula press the balls flat as you can. This is a very quick process. Give it around 10 seconds and flip both pattys. Add a touch of Maldon salt for seasoning.

Place the burger cheese on both pattys then lift one onto the other after about 20 seconds and take out the pan.

Assembly
On the toasted bun layer some mayonnaise on both the top and bottom of the buns. On the bottom add the pickle and onion mix – place the burger on top. Place the bacon on top of the burger and put the lid on. It should be a proper messy, juicy burger – enjoy!

El Perro Negro
152 Woodlands Road, G3 6LF
🌐 el-perro-negro.com
📷 elperronegroGLA

SARDINIAN
SEAFOOD SOUP

2 litres fish stock (homemade is of course better)

2 carrots, finely diced

2 stalks of celery, finely diced

½ white onion finely diced

½ bulb fennel (keep the fronds for garnish)

2 cloves of garlic, finely diced

1 sprig of fresh rosemary

1 sprig of sage

1 sprig of thyme

1 sprig of oregano

4 bay leaves

½ tsp orange zest

½ tsp lemon zest

3 tomatoes, diced

Salt & pepper

Dry white wine

1 tsp tomato puree

120g fregola, orzo or similar pasta

For the fish

Anything you have really. Preferably firm fish but it is essentially up to you.

We used: sea trout, hake, mackerel, mussels, clams.

"Born on a recent Hebridean break, this seafood soup is an easy, delicious and brings back memories of the Mediterranean." Colin Clydesdale

In a large saucepan lightly sautee the carrots, onions, fennel, celery and all fresh herbs in a little olive oil. After 8-10 minutes add the tomato puree, stir through, then add the white wine and stock.

Bring to the boil and add the pasta, turn down to a rolling simmer for about 5 minutes before adding your mussels, clams and prawns.

Keep simmering for another 5 minutes until all the mussels and clams are open. Discard any that stay closed.

Add the orange and lemon zest, fresh oregano and season to taste. Allow to rest while you cook the fish.

Sear your fillets in a hot frying pan, skin side down first for a couple of minutes either-side. Season lightly.

To serve, ladle the broth into bowls serving equal amounts of shellfish into each to avoid arguments.

Place the fish fillets on top and sprinkle with diced tomato, fennel fronds and a drizzle of olive oil.

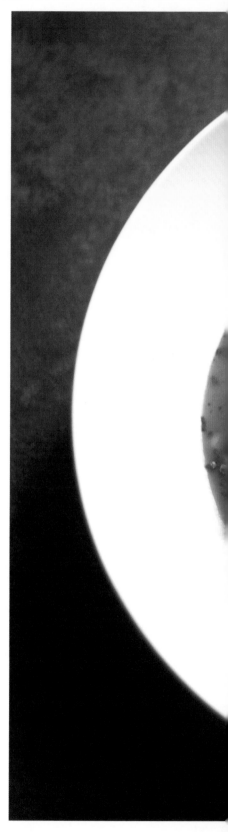

Ubiquitous Chip
12 Ashton Lane, G12 8SJ
🌐 ubiquitouschip.co.uk
📷 ubiquitous_chip

STEAMED MUSSELS
WITH CURRIED FENNEL & COCONUT MILK

1½ kilo mussels, washed & cleaned

2 onions, chopped

2 heads of fennel, finely sliced

1 tbsp ginger, chopped

1 tbsp garlic, chopped

2 red chillies, split

2 tbsp vegetable oil

2 tins chopped tomatoes

500ml coconut milk

2 tbsp white wine vinegar

100ml water

For the spice paste

2 tsp ground coriander

2 tsp ground cumin

2 tsp ground curry powder

½ tsp ground turmeric

½ tsp black pepper

2 tsp water

1 cinnamon stick

"Mussels are a more versatile shellfish than people think, and they hold their own here with the creamy, curried fennel sauce." *Derek Marshall, Head Chef*

To make the spice paste, put all the ingredients into a blender until you have a fine paste. Leave aside until required.

Heat the oil in a pan and add the onions, ginger, garlic and chilli. Fry until the onions turn translucent. Add the vinegar, spice paste and chopped tomatoes with the water. Cover the pan and cook over a low heat for 8-10 minutes then add the coconut milk and cook for a further 10 minutes.

In another pot, sweat off the fennel in a little butter until soft. Add the mussels and cover with a lid, after three minutes add the curry sauce and stir in thoroughly. Put the lid back on the pot and leave to cook, making sure the mussels have fully opened. If there are some mussels not fully opened, discard these.

Serve in warmed bowls and pour the fennel and curry sauce over the top.

Gamba
225A W George St, G2 2ND
gamba.co.uk
gambaglasgow

DIWANI HANDI

Serves 4

1kg lamb on the bone

2 medium-sized onions, chopped

40g ginger-garlic paste

100g chopped tomatoes

4-5 green cardamon pods

2 black cardamon pods, slightly crushed

5-6 cloves

5-6 black peppercorns

4 bay leaves

1 medium size cinnamon stick

1 tsp cumin seeds

75ml oil

1 tsp turmeric

1 tsp red chilli powder

1 tsp paprika

1/2 tsp ground coriander

1/2 tsp cumin powder

½ tbsp garam masala

25g salt

25g fresh coriander, chopped

VINCENZO SEVERINO

"Lamb on the bone, with aromatics and spices. Traditional rural cooking at its finest."

Heat the oil in flat-bottomed pan. Add green cardamon, black cardamom, cloves, black peppercorns, bay leaves, the cinnamon stick and cumin seeds.

After they start to crackle add the onions and saute until it browns.

Now add the ginger-garlic paste and turmeric. Once they start to roast add the tomato and salt.

After the tomatoes turn into a mash add the lamb and cook for about 5 minutes till the lamb starts turning dry.

Add the turmeric, red chilli powder, paprika, ground coriander, ground cumin and garam masala. Mix well and cook for a further 2-3 minutes.

Add 2 cups to hot water to the pan and cover.

Cook on low heat for about 30 minutes or till the lamb starts to become tender.

Sprinkle the chopped coriander on top.

Serve hot, with steamed basmati rice.

The Dhabba
44 Candleriggs, G1 1LD
🌐 thedhabba.com
📷 thedhabba

TURBOT TANDOORI
WITH SAMPHIRE RAITA, AND A SALT & VINEGAR POPPADOM

Serves two

For the cured turbot
100g brown sugar

50g salt

1 tsp cardamom powder

1 tsp cinnamon

1 tsp mild curry powder

1 lemon zest and juice

two 125g turbot fillets

1 box uncooked popadoms (or buy ready to eat to avoid frying at home)

Raita
25g samphire

25g cucumber, thinly sliced

2 large tablespoons natural yoghurt

5 mint leaves, torn

Fry poppadoms in 180°C oil until they double in size (or use pre-made).

Sprinkle with 1 tsp of MSK salt and vinegar powder (order online or pick up from a speciality supermarket).

Cure turbot for 4 hours. Remove the fish and pat dry with paper towel.

Fry in a hot pan on one side only for 2 mins until golden/lightly charred.

Flip and remove pan from heat.

Remove turbot from pan after 1 minute. Plate and garnish with baby red shiso leaves.

Five March
140 Elderslie St, G3 7QF
🌐 fivemarch.co.uk
📷 five_march

MICHAEL HUNTER

PAPPARDELLE WITH WILD BOAR RAGU

For the marinade

500ml of red wine

1 onion, roughly chopped

2 bay leaves

½ tbsp of juniper berries

3 cloves of garlic

2 sprigs of rosemary

For the ragu

800g of wild boar shoulder, diced

6 tblsp of olive oil

1 onion, finely diced

1 carrot, finely diced

1 stick of celery, finely diced

2 bay leaves

3 garlic cloves, finely sliced

400g of Italian tinned tomatoes or passata

2 tbsp of tomato puree

250ml of red wine

Salt & black pepper, to taste

Rinse wild boar meat in cold water, shake off any excess water and place in a large bowl.

Add all of the marinade ingredients to the bowl and thoroughly mix with the boar meat, cover and place in the fridge to marinate for 12 to 24 hours.

Once marinated, strain and discard all of the liquid, vegetables and herbs.

Put 4 tbsp of olive oil in a heavy pot or casserole, shake excess moisture from the meat, add to the pan and seal and brown on all sides.

Remove meat with a slotted spoon and reserve. Add the rest of the oil, onion, carrot, celery, garlic and bay leaves and fry for a few minutes without colouring.

Add the browned meat and its juices back into the pot along with the red wine and reduce for a couple of minutes, stirring occasionally so it doesn't stick.

Add a cup of water, the tomatoes and tomato puree and stir through, season with a good pinch each of salt and pepper and stir the ingredients together.

Put a lid on the pot and place in a preheated oven 170ºC/150ºC fan, for 2 to 2½ hours.

Take out occasionally and stir, add beef stock or a little water if it seems too dry.

Check for seasoning and serve with pappardelle pasta topped with grated parmesan cheese.

Sugo Pasta
70 Mitchell Street, G1 3LX
🌐 sugopasta.co.uk
📷 sugopastaglasgow

MICHAEL HUNTER

TANDOORI CHICKEN

1 whole chicken (1-1.2kg)

First marinade

2 tsp ginger and garlic paste
2 tsp red chilli powder (medium hot)
1 tbsp juice of lemon
1 tsp salt

Second marinade

2 tsp ginger and garlic paste
2 tsp turmeric powder
2 tsp coriander powder
2 tsp chaat masala
2 tbsp thick yogurt
2 tsp dried fenugreek leaves
Juice of a lemon
1 ½ tsp salt
2 tbsp mustard/vegetable oil

Note: Internal temperature should not be less than 75°C when ready and juices must run clear.

Prepare your chicken. Apply a deep slit right in the middle of the chicken breast where the breastbone is.

Apply a few deep slits on each chicken breast.

Apply deep slits on each leg of the chicken.

Mix all the ingredients of the first marinade and rub onto the chicken.

Mix all the ingredients of the second marinade and marinate the chicken well.

Let the chicken sit in the marinades overnight for the best results.

Pre-heat the oven to 200°C/180°C fan.

Put the chicken into an ovenproof dish and place on the middle shelf inside of the oven.

Cook it for 45 minutes to 1 hour uncovered and baste it with melted butter every 15 minutes.

Ensure that tandoori chicken roast is cooked well and let it rest for 10 minutes before serving.

Swadish
33 Ingram Street, G1 1HA
🌐 swadish.co.uk
📷 swadishmerchantcity

RAVIOLI GRANCHIO

For the ravioli

200 grams of flour

200g rimacinata flour (mixing the two types of flour together makes it tastier)

7 eggs

Pinch of salt

Crab

Dill

For the sauce

1 lobster

Butter

Cream

Shalotts

Parsley

Brandy

Salt & pepper

"Crab filled ravioli in a lobster claw meat sauce. This is one of our most popular dishes and has been on the menu at La Lanterna for 50 years. The secret behind the dish is the restaurant's homemade ravioli." *Luca Conreno, Head Chef*

Make the pasta dough by mixing the flour, eggs and a pinch of salt until the dough is soft and smooth. Cover it with a damp towel and let it rest for approximately an hour.

Use a pasta machine and create thin pasta sheets, and cut into ravioli squares using a ravioli maker.

Fill with the crab filling by using a spoon, close and seal the ravioli by using your fingers.

Boil the lobster and then remove the meat, claw and body.

Put the lobster in a pan with a spoon of butter, half a chopped shallot and chopped parsley then stir until light brown.

Add the chopped lobster to the pan and stir it carefully. Then add some brandy and a touch of cream.

Boil the ravioli, you will know that they are ready as soon as they come up to the surface of the water. Fresh ravioli should take about three minutes. Then drain and put the ravioli into the saucepan with the lobster.

A good tip is to use use some of the ravioli cooking water in the sauce.

Sprinkle some salt and pepper and chop some parsley.

Serve on a big plate using some of the clean lobster as decoration.

La Lanterna
35 Hope Street, G2 6AE
🌐 lalanterna-glasgow.co.uk
📷 lalanternaglasgow

BRAISED PIG CHEEKS
WITH GRILLED CHORIZO, CREAMED POLENTA

Serves 4

8-12 pig cheeks
12 chorizo slices
½ cup polenta
1 cup vegetable stock
1 cup cream
Truffle oil – to taste
1 pack of spinach
1 courgette
Tempura flour
2 onions
1 clove garlic
½ pack of thyme
100g butter
300ml chicken stock
300ml beef stock

Pre heat the oven to 180°C.

Wash the pig cheeks, and place in a ovenproof pot, colouring the cheeks all over with an even colour. Remove from the pot and get rid of the excess fat in the pot.

Peel and chop the onions roughly. Cut the garlic in half. Put the butter into the already used pot, add the onions and garlic and fry until a nice dark colour, add the pig cheeks, followed by the chicken and beef stock, dropping in the thyme leaves and bringing to the boil.

Put greaseproof paper on top of the pot and put into the oven for around 2 – 3 hours.

When cooked, take out of the stock, pass through a sieve to be left with the remaining vegetables and herbs in the sieve.

With the remaining vegetables and herbs put into a small pot and reduce down until a nice coating consistency is achieved.

Place the chorizo onto a tray, then put under the grill for a few minutes.

With the remaining stock, put into a pan, bring to the boil, add the polenta, mixing well for a few minutes until the polenta is cooked. If it's not creamy enough, just add a little more cream, adding truffle oil to suit your taste.

Wash and cook the spinach. Slice the courgette at a slight angle.

Mix some tempura flour with a little water, mixing well so it's nice and smooth. Put the courgette in the mix, drain then fry in the deep fat fryer, slowly until golden brown and crispy (these are known as courgette beignets).

Dressing the plate
Put the polenta onto the base of the plate, then add a little spinach, placing the pig cheek on top, place a couple of the chorizo pieces and courgette beignets over the cheek, then drizzle the sauce over and around.

**Brian Maule
at Chardon d'Or**
176 W Regent St, G2 4RL
🌐 brianmaule.com
📷 lechardon_dor

COLIN MEARNS

GANDOLFI'S CULLEN SKINK

Serves 4

4 medium potatoes, peeled & diced

300ml double cream

300ml whole milk

250ml water

300g smoked haddock

60g butter

1 onion, finely chopped

1 tbsp olive oil

Pinch of mace or nutmeg

Black pepper

In a saucepan large enough to take all the ingredients, sauté the onion in butter and oil until soft.

Add the water to the pan along with the potatoes and simmer for 5 minutes.

Stir in the milk and cream and simmer for a further 5-10 minutes until the potatoes are tender.

Cut the haddock into 2cm squares and drop into the soup. Continue to cook gently for 10 minutes.

Check seasoning and add the mace or nutmeg.

Cafe Gandolfi
64 Albion Street, G1 1NY
🌐 cafegandolfi.com
📷 cafegandolfi

SONYA WALOS

AGED BEEF & SMOKED EEL
WITH KOHLRABI

120g aged shorthorn

20g beef dripping

1 chipping potato (Maris Piper)

20g clarified butter

1 kohlrabi

150g smoked eel (bone & skin attached)

For the mayonnaise

30g pasteurized egg yolks

15g dijon mustard

15g white wine vinegar

300ml eel infused sunflower oil

salt

lemon juice

10g water

"I hope you enjoy making this dish as much as I did. It's proven to be immensely popular since we started serving it to our guests at The Gannet" *Peter McKenna, Chef and Co-Owner*

Melt the dripping in a pan, season then sear the outside of the beef evenly, chill in the fridge.

Fillet the eel, remove the skin and be careful to cut out the pin bones (you could ask a fishmonger for help or advice).

Dice the fillet and store in the fridge.

Infuse the eel bones and skin in the sunflower oil in a pan over a low heat, 30-45 minutes, once it's taken on sufficient smoked eel flavour, take it out of the pan and chill.

To make mayonnaise with the chilled eel oil, add egg yolk, Dijon and vinegar to the blender. Slowly add the oil until all is incorporated, add a splash of water if required. Season with salt and lemon juice, and store in a squeezing bottle or piping bag.

Peel and slice the potato (very fine), in a bowl add clarified butter and mix, on a baking tray lined with greaseproof spread into individual circles (large enough to cover the beef) use a large ring mould. Once you have made the required shapes cover with more greaseproof paper and a heavy tray. Bake in the oven at 180ºC for 8 – 10 minutes, all ovens are different, so please check after 5 minutes.

Once cooked and golden remove from the hot tray and dry on some paper towels.

Peel the kohlrabi, use half for batons, weigh and add 2% of its weight in salt, leave for 5 minutes then rinse off.

With the other half slice thinly and cut into circles, keep fresh in ice water.

To assemble:

Slice the beef evenly.

Use the rings from the potatoes and fit the beef in on a nice plate evenly.

Once all plates have an equal amount of beef on them and are neat and tidy, season with sea salt (I prefer Blackthorn from Ayrshire).

Pipe the mayonnaise onto the beef as we do in the restaurant or use less if you'd like.

Add the diced eel and kohlrabi sticks and discs.

Top with the crisp potato.

Garnish with some nice edible flowers or mild leaves, there is a lot of flavour in the dish so be careful not to add any more aggressive flavours.

The Gannet
1155 Argyle St, G3 8TB
🌐 thegannetgla.com
📷 thegannetgla

SONYA WALDS

SONYA WALOS

APPLE, ALMOND & COCONUT CAKE

2 apples, peeled, cored & diced

zest of one lemon

juice of a half a lemon

6 eggs

225g caster sugar

240g ground almonds

1 tsp gluten-free baking powder

½ tsp vanilla extract

40g flaked almonds

A handful of coconut shavings

For the coconut buttercream

280g icing sugar

100g softened unsalted butter

3 tbsp coconut milk

"This lovely moist cake is a great gluten-free treat and, providing gluten-free baking powder is used (available to buy in the 'free from' aisle in any large supermarket), and it is suitable for coeliacs." *Nichola Reith*

Place the apples in a pan along with lemon juice and zest and cook on a low heat until softened (about 15 – 20 minutes). Set aside to cool.

Grease and line an 8" tin and pre-heat the oven to 160°C

Whisk the eggs and sugar together.

Stir in the cooled apples.

Add the ground almonds, baking powder, vanilla and flaked almonds and stir until all ingredients are well combined.

Pour the cake mixture into the prepared tin and bake for 40 mins. After 40 minutes check the cake by inserting a skewer into the cake, if it comes out clean the cake is ready. If not, give the cake another 10 minutes in the oven.

To make the buttercream whisk the icing sugar and butter together until light and fluffy. Add the coconut milk and whisk for another minute.

Once the cake has cooled, turn it out of the tin and top with buttercream

Finally sprinkle with coconut shavings.

Cake Bar
401 Gt. Western Rd, G4 9HY
🌐 cakebaruk.com
📷 cakebar_uk

ONE BIG PICTURE PHOTOGRAPHY

ROASTED MONKFISH
WITH LENTIL DAHL, MASALA PICKLED ONIONS, CAULIFLOWER, & A YELLOW PEPPER SAUCE

2 monkfish tails
1 tbsp curry powder
2 limes
Fresh Coriander

For the dahl
200g red lentils
400g tin coconut milk
1 lemongrass stalk, split
2 cloves garlic, peeled & crushed
10g ginger, sliced
pinch of fennel seeds
pinch of coriander seeds
2 cardamom pods
mint leaves
fresh coriander
50ml vegetable oil

Yellow pepper sauce
4 yellow peppers
130g coconut milk
60ml white wine
1 shallot, sliced
1 clove of garlic, peeled & halved
pinch of curry powder
1 tbsp butter

Golden raisins
50g golden raisins
100ml water
20g salt

Onions
Selection of small baby onions or shallots
125ml white wine vinegar
200ml water
50g sugar
1 tbsp Masala curry powder
pinch of coriander seeds

Roasted cauliflower
1 cauliflower, cut into florets & cut in half (approx. 4 – 6 florets)
curry powder
2 tbsp. butter
1 floret for raw shaving

"I love Indian food and occasionally like to move away from the classics and experiment with spices. This is a dish which is always on the menu at some point throughout the year at One Devonshire gardens. I'm aware that monkfish isn't readily available in a lot of supermarkets so you could substitute this with cod. A good wee tip for checking if monkfish is cooked is by taking a cocktail stick and sticking it through the fish. If it slides through with ease then your fish is cooked, any resistance then you will need another minute or so." *Gary Townsend, Head Chef*

Pre heat oven to 180°C, gas mark 4.

First, to prepare the pickled onions, you need to bring the vinegar, water, sugar, coriander seeds and curry powder to the boil. Peel the onions if needed. Place them in an airtight, sterilised glass jar and pour over the liquid. Allow to cool and seal. This will start the pickling process. The longer they are left in the jar the better the result will be. These will last for around 6 weeks.

Similar to the onions, the raisins are better soaked a day ahead. Place all the ingredients in a pan, bring to the boil then remove from the heat and allow to cool in the liquor. Place in an airtight container until needed. These will keep for around 6 weeks also.

For the monkfish, remove the meat from either side of the bone and trim away any excess skin and membrane, a fishmonger will do this for you. Wash and pat dry – set aside.

To make the yellow pepper sauce, juice the peppers if you have a juicer, if not, blend in a food processor and pass through a fine sieve. Next, in a medium sized pan sweat off shallots and garlic, add the curry powder and season. Add the wine and reduce to syrup then add pepper juice, cook on a medium heat for around 5 minutes then add the coconut milk. Allow to infuse for 10 minutes then pass through a sieve, add the butter and whisk together.

For the dahl, heat the oil in a medium sized pan on a low heat with lemongrass, garlic, ginger, coriander seeds, fennel seeds and cardamom. Heat these slowly for around 5-10minutes. This flavours the oil that the lentils will be cooked in.

Let the oil cool slightly, pass through a metal sieve into a container. Place the oil back in the pan with the lentils stirring them through the oil, heat gently for 2 minutes followed by the coconut milk and 2 stems of mint. Cook this on a low heat until the lentils have soaked up all of the coconut milk, you can add more if you feel it needs it. Check for seasoning and remove the mint stem.

For the roasted cauliflower, heat a small amount of oil in a frying pan on a medium heat. Dust each flat side of the floret in curry powder then gently lay into the pan. Season with a little salt and cook until a golden brown colour. Add the butter and lower the heat. Continue to cook until soft. Remove from the pan and drain on a paper towel.

For the cooking of the monkfish have a pan on a medium heat with a small amount of oil. Season the monkfish lightly with salt then dust it with the curry powder. Lower the fish carefully in the pan colouring each side before finishing in the oven for around 4- 5 minutes depending on the size. Finish with a squeeze of lime juice.

Build your dish with the lentil dahl at the bottom, with your fish on top. Add your cauliflower florets followed by a scattering of raisins and onions and raw shaved cauliflower. Finish with some fresh coriander and lime zest!

One Devonshire Gardens
1 Devonshire Gardens, Glasgow G12 0UX
🌐 hotelduvin.com/locations/glasgow/
📷 hotelduvinglasgow

DRY-AGED STEAK CARPACCIO
WITH CHORIZO & BLACK PUDDING STUFFED MUSHROOM, HORSERADISH & PARMESAN TUILE, CURED EGG YOLK

Serves 4

For the stuffed mushrooms
4 chestnut mushrooms
1 garlic clove
50g butter
100g black pudding
60g chorizo

For the fillet carpaccio
240g fillet tail
100 ml olive oil
15g pink peppercorns
1 tsp Dijon mustard
1 sprig thyme
1 garlic clove

For the tuile
50g horseradish
140g parmesan

For the salt-cured egg yolk
4 eggs
200g kosher salt
140g sugar

Salt-cured egg yolk

Take your kosher salt and sugar and fold together. Next, take half the mix, place on a baking tray and make 4 small egg yolk-sized wells in your mix.

Separate the yolk from the white, discarding the whites, and gently place each yolk into the wells.

Cover each egg yolk with remaining salt mix and set aside for 2 hours.

After 2 hours, take yolks and individually rinse gently under cold water.

Fillet Carpaccio

In a bowl, combine the olive oil, Dijon mustard, thyme and garlic until mixed well. Separately, make the spice rub by crushing the pink peppercorns then pour onto a tray.

Trim away any sinew from the fillet then massage in the olive oil rub. Once well coated, roll the fillet through crushed peppercorns, ensuring full coverage. Allow 20 minutess for flavours to infuse with the meat and to bring meat up to room temperature.

Place the fillet in a hot pan to sear the outside only, ensuring the middle of the steak is cooked blue.

Slice the fillet as thinly as possible, about 2 to 3 mm. Place the slices between 2 sheets of parchment paper and go over with rolling pin.

Store in fridge until ready to be served.

Parmesan & Horseradish Tuile

Pre-heat oven to 180°C.

Finely grate your parmesan and horseradish, mix well.

On parchment paper, roll out mix no more than 2mm thick and cut out 4 discs using a 3" cutter.

Bake in oven for 6 mins, then take them out and leave to cool for 2 minutes.

Roll the cooling mix into a small cylinder and leave to set.

Stuffed Mushroom

Place your chorizo in a dry pan and allow to sweat down until all the oils are released. Then add the black pudding, cook until combined then place aside.

Keep oven heated to 180°C.

Remove stems and peel the mushrooms.

In a hot pan, melt the butter and add the garlic clove, and after a minute, toss the mushroom until coated in the garlic butter and set aside to cool.

Take your chorizo and black pudding mix and stuff the garlic mushrooms. Once all evenly stuffed place on a baking tray and place in the oven to cook for 6 mins.

Remove stuffed mushrooms from oven and spread between 4 plates immediately along with all other dish components to serve.

Porter & Rye
1131 Argyle St, G3 8ND
🌐 porterandrye.com
📷 porterandrye

Kelvingrove Park

A tranquil scene in Kelvingrove Park with local landmarks appearing through the trees. For more food and drink news, local recommendations, interviews and profiles, join us at *Glasgowist.com* all through the year and comment at *facebook.com/Glasgowist*